OTHERWISE

{ *A Collection of Stories Most People Would Keep to Themselves* }

UNTOLD

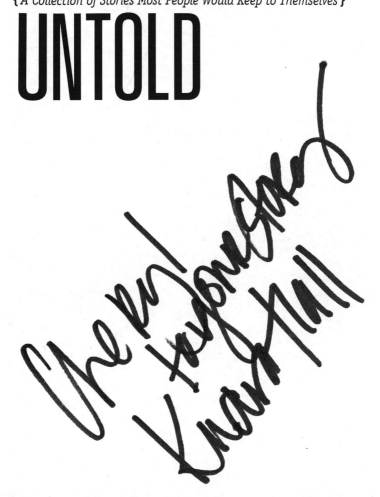

OTHERWISE

{ *A Collection of Stories Most People Would Keep to Themselves* }

UNTOLD

by **KINDRA HALL**

Phoenix

©2013 Telzall LLC

Cover design and layout by Sarah Sandhaus of Electric Dreams Design.
Printed in the United States of America

ISBN 978-0-9889987-0-4

To Michael

Who is even better in person than he is on these pages.

Author's Note

My stories have always been simple.
Regular things, happening on regular days to a regular girl.
It's easy to forget stories like these, to wait for your life to give you bigger ones.

I've never been very patient.
I decided to tell my stories now.

OTHERWISE UNTOLD

THE YEAR OF TITANIC

It was the year of the *Titanic*.

That ill-destined ship and little blue-haired lady rocked my world and the world of millions. You couldn't go anywhere without the sound of teenage girls screaming *Leeeoooo. Leeeoooo.* Theaters sold out for weeks—I knew a girl who went eleven times. *Eleven* times. She had to get a second job to pay for her obsession. Every talk show, every newspaper, every television commercial break had visions of the sinking masterpiece, a crying redheaded woman and a young man too beautiful to survive the tragic event. And on every radio station you could hear the haunting flute and the unforgettable wail of Celine Dion as she belted out the ballad that would top the charts for what seemed like a decade.

The *Titanic* Phenomenon began the winter of my junior year of high school. A time of love. A time of pain. A time of two mismatched souls who, though it was all wrong, found each other, only to have it end all too soon.

In fact, *Titanic was* my junior year of high school.

The year of David.

• • • • •

It started the way most high school love stories do.

It was the first day of class my junior year. My best friend Stephanie and I had already taken our seats in Modern Lit and we watched the door as various juniors and seniors filed in. Some I liked, some I didn't know, some who were way too cool, some who wore capes and pretended they were wizards in the cafeteria before Harry Potter was born, and one who I had seen before— but never remembered him looking like *that*...

Like *hot*.

His name was David. He was a senior. He had light skin,

blue eyes, blond curly hair, and clear braces. He was the quarterback of the football team, second baseman on the baseball team, and center on the basketball team. He was smart enough to be on the math team and cool enough to be on student council, but did neither.

My heart skipped a beat as he scanned the room for an open seat, walked my way, and took the last remaining desk... the one right in front of *me*. As he passed by, the air he left behind was sweetened with the smell of Joop!.

This was going to be the best semester of my life.

• • • • •

To be honest, I'm not sure how I pulled it off. I was notorious for scaring boys with my dramatic behavior, over-the-top plots, and loud conversation—all common characteristics of a storyteller on the high school speech team, which I was. However, when it came to David, I really tried. I tried to be cool, tried to be attractive, tried to hide my storyteller-ness.

To my surprise, it worked.

By November 17 (according to my eleventh-grade diary), after months of casually attending every football game

that didn't interfere with the school play or a speech
meet, only buying gas at Wally's Gas Station on the days
that David worked, trying to use my inside voice and not
move my eyebrows so much when I talked, David and I
went on our first date.

And I was in love.
A storyteller. In love. With the quarterback.
This story *couldn't* end well.

That fall was filled with secret "friend" dates. We'd meet
up after games and watch movies at my parents' house.
We'd do our *Hondo* and *Brave New World* homework
from Modern Lit together when no one was looking.
We went to school dances—arriving separately, leaving
separately, and barely talking to each other in between.
I loved his company when I had it. Even if he stood on
the other side of the gymnasium pretending he didn't
know me, it didn't matter because I knew better; I knew,
against all odds, we were meant to be.

Then, the night of the first snow, after a party at a
friend's house we attended separately, we walked to my
car... Together.

I noticed we were walking slower than everyone else. By

the time we got to my station wagon, it was covered in three inches of new snow.

I noticed David was more than willing to clean it off for me as he watched all his friends—football players, basketball players, baseball players—drive away.
I noticed when we were alone.
And I *really* notice when he came toward me.
Close enough that under the streetlight I could see big snowflakes resting on his blond lashes.
Then close enough that I could see the blue of his eyes.
Then close enough that even under his letterman jacket I could smell Joop!.

Then close enough that I wondered... if I just closed my eyes...

And then he kissed me. Straight out of a fairytale.

The next several months were filled with the ups and downs of a teenage relationship. Movies, sporting events, prom, playing Nintendo 64 Bond 007, Pizza Man, holding hands, kissing on the couches of various basements, navigating clear braces, notes in lockers, midnight curfews, driving way too fast on dirt roads to make it home before the midnight curfews, cheering at basketball games and baseball games. Many breakups, multiple makeups, and of course there was *Titanic*.

I saw *Titanic* once. With David. We probably went to Olive Garden first. I tried not to cry and tried to hold David's hand. Both attempts were unsuccessful.

Then, when assigned to do a spoof on a movie for our Spanish class, we did *Titanic*. Even though David wasn't in the class, and even though David didn't speak Spanish, I forced him to participate. David was Juan, I was Rosa, the drowning scene happened in a hot tub with swimsuits, the steamy car scene was created with a humidifier and David read off cue cards.

And for Valentine's Day, David wrapped the *Titanic* soundtrack in a brown paper lunch bag. He wrote "To Kindra" in red marker and "Love David" in purple. It was the first, the only time he used the word *Love* and with that gesture, *My Heart Will Go On* would always be our song. And even though we broke up (again) the next day, that night the Quarterback and the Storyteller slow danced in his basement.

While David and I were certainly compatible—both intelligent, both driven, both good at what we did—among the rules and regulations of high school, we were on a sinking ship. At the end of the school year we broke up for the last time when he kissed a girl from the dance team. She seemed to be a better fit.

It was the end of the Storyteller and the Quarterback.

I remember sitting at the kitchen table, my eyes red and puffy from crying. It was over and my heart was broken. I had spent the entire school year trying to be someone I wasn't—hiding my talents, ashamed of my skills, determined to be something other, something better, than a *storyteller*. None of it was good enough. My mother sat next to me and I asked her, seventeen years old, breathless and desperate, how I could ever turn the radio on again. I would never be able to escape that song... never be able to escape David, escape my broken heart, escape who I wanted to be but couldn't.

My mother pushed the hair off my tear-soaked face and with her infinite wisdom said, "Oh Kindra, you must believe me when I say this. Someday you will hear that song and smile."

• • • • •

It started as many adult love stories do. Over email.

Somewhere between 1998 and 2003 David and I managed to reconnect via happy birthday emails exchanged
twice a year within weeks of each other. This led to
phone conversations and eventually my first dinner at a
Thai restaurant.

Where we picked up was better than where we left off.

David was working at some computer company doing
something with programming that I didn't understand.
But he was thinking of leaving, thinking of getting his
law degree. He looked the same to me—light skin, blue
eyes, blond curly hair, and a smile that was worth
the braces.

I had just finished my master's degree and at the end
of the summer I was moving to Arizona to head up the
southwest operations of a Minnesota-based title and
escrow company. I didn't have to pretend to be cool; I
knew it all sounded good. Official. Fancy. Not the least
bit like something a *storyteller* would be doing. He
seemed impressed.

We spent some time together that summer, being the
friends we never allowed ourselves to be in high school.
And though there was no prom, no kissing, and no

Celine, my heart was healed.

We went our separate ways, he to Pepperdine, me to Scottsdale, and stayed in touch. I was one of the first to congratulate him on his law degree and in 2008, when it came time to send out the invitations to my wedding, David was on the list. We danced at the reception, he told me the groom was a lucky man, and paid for the cab that took my new husband and I home that night.

• • • • •

Since our dinner at Thai, I had worked my way up. From a failed stint at the title company that never opened in Arizona, to a beer cart girl on an Arizona golf course, to director of marketing, and eventually promoted to vice president of sales, I was pretty impressed with what this "storyteller" (formerly destined to read books to children in libraries), had made of herself. Yet, as the years went on in those fancy titles, I became unsettled. I knew something was missing, something wasn't right.

• • • • •

In July 2010, I got an email from my old friend David. He needed a favor. He asked if I was willing to be a reference for him for some law license thing. Since I had secretly identified his parents as my emergency contacts in college, I figured I owed him. All he needed

was my address, daytime phone, and occupation—he
told me to list my favorite professional title. I wrote back
immediately with the info he wanted and included "Vice
President of Sales" as my occupation. He thanked me
and, almost as an afterthought, wrote:

*"I really wanted to list your title as Professional Story-
teller... but Vice President of Sales works as well."*

I read the email on my iPhone while straightening my
hair and putting on mascara on my way out the door to
the office.
I dropped everything.
I read it again.
And again, desperate to distinguish the sarcasm from
the serious. He couldn't be serious. He couldn't actually
mean that on his *official* file in some *official* law office
wanted there to be record of a "professional storyteller"
as his reference. No way. Sure, we weren't in high school
anymore, but come on.

I put on my professional heels, jumped in my fancy car,
and drove far too fast to work while I rehearsed what
I would write next. It was no different than the many
rough-drafts of "do you like me" notes I wrote for him in
eleventh grade. When I pulled into the parking lot at the

office I was shaking but prepared.

I texted him. "I sensed your sarcasm re 'professional storyteller.' "

I held my breath.
He wrote right back.

"No. I'm serious. I think that sounds a lot cooler than VP of Sales."

There, in my fancy car with my fancy shoes and fancy title in the parking lot of my fancy job...

I cried.
I knew exactly why.

I had invested years into running from myself—running from the fact that, at my core, in my soul, I am a *storyteller.* I cringe when I say it out loud. I still try to talk my way around it when someone asks me about it. I sound embarrassed, I sound nervous, I sound like a junior in high school who isn't cool enough to date the quarterback. Yet it haunts me. No matter how I try to hide, I always seem to find myself... and I'm always, a storyteller. It took David. David who was the first person I tried to "re-create" myself for, David who, at least *now* if not *all along*, simply wanted me to be myself. I knew it was time to stop hiding.

I decided to make a change.

Over the course of the next several months I left the fancy job and surrendered the fancy title to focus all of my time and energy on stories. I decided to become a storyteller. Was I nervous? Yes. Did I still stumble when people asked me what I do? Yes. Was I scared I wouldn't be happy?

No.

I'd never been happier.

• • • • •

It was one of my last full days at the office and I was driving home with the top down. I had my radio on some easy listening station when I heard a vaguely familiar sound; a haunting flute melody and an unforgettable wail. It was Celine. Suddenly I was seventeen and sitting at the kitchen table with my mother.

My mother who was right.

I turned the volume up and couldn't help but smile.

THE WOMAN BEHIND THE COUNTER

I was in the Phoenix Airport. Unsure of how long it would take to get the car parked, get the luggage checked, get through the security line, and get to the gate, I ended up at the airport early. So, I did what I always do when I'm early to the airport; I headed toward the newsstand for the sole purpose of staring at the tabloid magazine covers. I never buy, I *only* read the covers (and even in those few moments I can feel my brain cells rotting).

However, on this particular trip to the newsstand I witnessed something much more fascinating, and disturbing, than any tabloid could offer.

In the newsstand was a friendly looking gentleman. He had a pleasant face with a cheerful smile. He and I were hovering in the same area; I was looking at the magazines, he was looking at the Snickers bars, though "looking" wouldn't be the right word—"agonizing over" would be better. Sadly this friendly looking man was about two hundred pounds from healthy. As we stood silently by each other, I could hear him as he struggled to breathe, shifting uncomfortably from foot to foot as he worked his way down the candy display.

I watched him out of the corner of my eye as he picked up a regular-sized Snickers bar with his right hand and a king-sized Snickers with his left. He looked at his two options, back and forth, back and forth. He rolled them around in his hands, crinkled their wrappers, contemplating his decision. After at least a minute, he reached to put the regular-sized one back... a shame, I thought. He was so close.

But then, like a flash of lightning from above, at the very last moment, he threw the king-sized Snickers down. It landed atop the gum with a deafening THUD. The man turned and looked at me with regular Snickers in his hand, gripped it tightly, shrugged, and smiled.

For a moment, I glimpsed pride on his face, the kind of pride that comes from taking control of your life. Granted, it wasn't the best decision, but it was a step in the right direction and it was clear he was pleased with himself. I smiled back and nodded; a silent congratulations for a job well done.

He took his regular-sized Snickers and strutted to the register where a fiftyish woman waited. She was friendly in an abrasive sort of way, and as I moved to look at the cover of *Men's Health* I heard her say to the man (who was still in the glow of his recent victory):

"Sure you don't want the KING-sized Snickers? Looks awful good..."

The man, who had just made a good decision, froze. He stared at the woman behind the counter. In that moment, all the bustle of the Phoenix Airport stopped. As he stared at the abrasive woman, I stared at *him*. The woman reached for the king-sized Snickers and waved it in front of his face. "Don't do it. Don't do it," I willed him. But in the next moment, he nodded, took the king-sized Snickers, paid, and slowly walked away.

I wanted to say something, but it wasn't my place. As he

walked past, he didn't look my way; instead he looked to the ground and to the king-sized decision he held in his hand.

It would be easy to blame the woman behind the counter for the demise of my Snickers-loving friend. She didn't *have* to offer him the king-sized when he seemed to be perfectly content. However, it is not her fault; she was only doing her job (I swear they get paid on commission). No, the responsibility lies solely with the man who ultimately made the choice.

I relate to this man. In many ways I *am* this man. Whether in struggles with weight, or financial decisions, or whatever the vice may be, I had been there before; on the brink of a breakthrough, only to fall one good decision short by no fault other than my own.

• • • • •

It is in these times I remind myself, "Who I am now does not determine who I will be."

The difference between who I am now and who I will be happens because of choice. It doesn't have to be a heroic choice; it can be small, consistent choices made every day in the right direction that make the difference. But they must be made and can only be made by me.

• • • • •

And even as I make these good decisions, there is a good chance that others will continue to see me as I am now. That's OK. It's not their fault. They may not be aware that I have made a decision to change; not aware that I am making small consistent decisions toward the person I want to become. They may not see those small decisions or realize they are adding up. Regardless, I owe it to myself to stay focused.

This is where I believe the man at the candy counter went astray: He was making a small decision in the right direction, but when he got to the counter, the abrasive woman saw him as he *was*, not as the man he was *becoming*. Instead of staying focused he crumbled with the words, "I will always be this" ringing in his defeated ears.

I left the newsstand that day with no snacks or magazines, but instead with a renewed commitment to always act on behalf of my future self—and an understanding that I must always beware of the woman behind the counter.

THE PARABLE
OF THE EAGLE

It was Friday night and I was joining my friend Amy
for a small gathering at her home. Even though I didn't
see her often, I had always liked Amy. She was perky,
fun, and a little spacey. Above all else, she had always
been extremely positive and I just felt good when I was
around her.

I was the first to arrive and Amy and I talked as we set
the table for dinner, and though everything seemed as
it always had been, I couldn't help the feeling that Amy
was a little different than I remembered. I couldn't quite
put my finger on it, but before I had any more time for
analysis, her other guests arrived—friends from her
work, no one I'd met before.

The evening progressed the way it does with women; we ate, we drank, we chatted, we cleaned up. As I sat with Amy and her guests, I noticed the same "difference" in Amy that I had suspected earlier in the evening, only this time it was much more pronounced. It seemed as if her formerly positive attitude had been replaced by complaints and whining (for lack of a better word). She was filled with skepticism, a thirst for gossip, and convinced that everything was a conspiracy. Sitting up close and personal with "the new Amy" it was clear what had happened. I quickly did the math.

It had been four months since the last time I had seen Amy. In that time, Amy had started a new job, and by the time we had gathered at her home that night, she had been working there for three and a half months. Every day she walked into the office, and took her seat right next to two of the women who were now at Amy's home—two of the most rotten women I had ever met. That night I listened for hours about why their jobs sucked, and why so-and-so is such a (insert bad word here), and why this guy shouldn't have gotten the job, and why that woman got a different job even though she was under-qualified (it was because she slept with the boss—that's what they were spreading around the office at least), and how their department should get more money, and how they are the only three in the whole office who do anything, and about their uncomfortable desk chairs...

Without a pause they barreled through a well-rehearsed checklist of negativity.

It was painful to watch.

I wanted to shake Amy, to say, *"Snap out of it! They have put a spell on you! You must retreat!"* But I knew there was nothing I could do.

As long as Amy spent eight hours a day with these women, there was not much that *anyone* could do...

Because, for better or worse...

We are the average of the five people we spend the most time with.

Our attitudes, our beliefs, our ambitions, our outlook; in most cases they are simply the *average* of the five people we spend the most time with. Never had this universal fact been clearer than sitting at Amy's that Friday night.

An hour later I excused myself and as Amy hugged me goodbye, I felt a wave of sadness. Sadness because I knew that, until Amy stopped spending so much of her time with those women from work or started spending *more* time with others, I may never know her as the friend she used to be.

Thinking about the evening, on the drive home I recalled a parable I had heard once before. A parable first told in the 1920s by James Aggrey. Here is the story as I remember it:

––––––––––––––––––

Once there was a farmer who was walking through the forest where the trees were so tall they touched the sky. As the farmer walked he came across a small bird, a baby eagle, wandering and lost on the ground beneath the branches. The farmer, being a kind man, decided to help the bird. He scooped him up and brought him home to raise him...

As one of his chickens.

The baby eagle, King of the Sky, called a chicken coop his home.

Every morning the farmer would come out to the coop to feed the chickens. He would toss seed to the birds. The chickens would peck at the ground and the eagle would peck at the ground. The chickens would cluck and clatter and the eagle would cluck and clatter. The chickens would wiggle their tails and the eagle would wiggle his tail. The chickens never raised their wings so the eagle never knew he *had* wings.... And the eagle *never* looked to the sky. Why would he? He was a chicken.

One day a wise man happened to be passing through and came across the farmer's home with the chicken coop and noticed the eagle. The King of the Sky, a vision of freedom and greatness, was trapped with a flock of common birds. The wise man spoke to the farmer, "My friend, what is this eagle, this King of the Sky doing pecking at the ground like a chicken? Eagles are meant to soar."

The farmer looked at the wise man, confused. "No sir, that's not an eagle. That there's a chicken. Walks like a chicken. Talks like a chicken. Eats like a chicken. That there's a chicken."

The wise man shook his head; it was wrong, so wrong. He begged the farmer for the opportunity to prove that this bird was in fact an eagle. The farmer nodded and the wise man placed the eagle on his arm saying, "You are an *eagle*. You are the King of the Sky. Now FLY!"

The eagle looked at the wise man with his dark eyes. If

he was going to fly, this was the moment.

But the moment was cut short. Just then the farmer pulled out his bag of seed and began tossing it to the chickens, which began pecking at the ground. The eagle hopped from the arm of the wise man and joined the chickens, pecking the ground for his food.

The farmer, without even looking at the wise man said, "See, I told you. That there's a chicken."

The next day the wise man returned, refusing to accept this eagle as a chicken and begged the farmer for another chance to make the eagle fly. The farmer, though skeptical, agreed. This time the wise man placed the eagle on his arm as he climbed to the top of the barn. There, many feet in the air, the wise man spoke to the bird.

"You are an *eagle*. You are the King of the Sky. You are not meant to be bound to the earth, you are meant to soar." The wise man reached out his arm and the eagle looked at him. In those glassy eyes the wise man thought he saw a glimmer of the greatness he knew this bird to be... but at that moment, the farmer stood in the chicken coop with a bag of seed and began to toss it to the chickens.

The chickens pecked at the ground.
The eagle hopped down to join them.

The very next day the wise man returned for a final time
and begged the farmer, "Farmer, dear farmer, please. I
know this is an eagle."

The farmer responded, "Wise man, you are not that
wise. How many times do I have to tell you—that there's
a chicken. Walks like a chicken, talks like a chicken,
eats like a chicken."

The wise man pleaded for one more chance and the
farmer finally agreed. This time the wise man took the
eagle and climbed to the top of one of the trees in the
forest that touched the sky. He pulled the bird in close
and whispered,

"You. *You are an eagle.* You are *destined* for great things.
I know this may be hard for you to believe since you
spend all your time with chickens but please, please you
must trust me. You are the King of the Sky. You were
not meant to peck at the ground but to soar above the
earth; a symbol of freedom and endless possibility. The

time has come for you to say goodbye to the chickens, the time has come for you to *FLY*."

The eagle looked to the wise man. Far below he could hear the farmer throwing feed to the chickens. And while he may have been tempted, just then the wind picked up. It kissed the chocolate brown feathers on the wings of that majestic bird—wings he had never seen before, wings he slowly, carefully spread to their full span. With a cry, the eagle leapt from the arm of the wise man and seized the sky.

The sky that was always his to have.
And he disappeared among the clouds.

We do not know if the eagle ever thinks back fondly of his time with the chickens, but we *do* know he never returned. He was an eagle. The King of the Sky. The time had come for him to leave the life of chickens and *live* like the king he was.

Our lives are filled with chickens; people with no aspirations to fly, like the women in the office where my friend Amy spent most of her time. Our lives are filled with farmers; well-meaning individuals who misread our potential. And while there are certainly wise men in our midst and we are grateful when they find us, there is no reason we should wait to be found. If you suspect you are an eagle, and you suspect you might be living among chickens, flee the coop. Spend time with people who spend no time pecking at the ground because they are far too busy reaching for the sky. Flee the chicken coop and seek out other eagles with whom to soar.

CHICKEN À LA KINDRA

I had just signed a lease on a beautiful one-bedroom apartment. And while I should have been thrilled, I had mixed feelings.

A one-bedroom apartment makes one of two statements. Statement A: I live with my significant other and we love each other so much that we prefer extremely close quarters. Statement B: I live by myself with no significant other. Additionally, none of my friends want to live with me, otherwise I would have gotten a two-bedroom apartment and a roommate.

Statement A didn't apply to me.

However, a benefit to my one-bedroom apartment meant I would never have to waste a moment on cooking because I would never have to worry about supplying a satisfying meal for anyone but myself, and for me Lean Cuisine was satisfying enough. Every night, a different delectable dish that needed no more than seven minutes maximum in the microwave. Sesame Chicken, Macaroni and Cheese, Lasagna, Three Cheese Ravioli, all perfect for my one-bedroom apartment and me.

Then one day, I met a guy. I wanted to impress said guy. Looking back, I think all I would have had to do is tie my shoe in front of him, but I didn't know that at the time. I decided to invite him out to dinner. But, instead of going out to a fancy dinner, which I couldn't really do because rent on the one bedroom apartment was a little steep, I decided I would cook.

I have no idea what I was thinking.

It was the day of our date and I knew I was going to have to make something happen. I considered cooking a few Lean Cuisines and putting them in bowls to make it *look* like home cooking, but I didn't have two of the same kind and two *different* home cooked meals might look suspicious. I looked online for a recipe that I might be able to handle. I found one on a site called something like "You Should Have Gone Out for Dinner." It involved chicken, mushroom soup, apricots, toothpicks and some other ingredients I had only vaguely heard of before. I immediately began taking my kitchen apart looking for what the recipe needed and within moments the kitchen was a war zone. Chicken breasts everywhere, mushroom soup in my hair... it wasn't good. To top it off, I apparently didn't have the right pan (or pot?). It was all too much for me. I needed a break.

I walked into the living room of my beautiful one-bedroom apartment and collapsed on the floor. I grasped for the remote and turned on the television. The talk show with all the women sitting around and yapping was on... it did well to drown out the voice inside my head saying *FAILURE*.

On this particular day Cyndi Lauper was the featured guest. Cyndi Lauper has been a household name for decades with songs as memorable as *Girls Just Wanna Have Fun*, that weird song at the beginning of the *Goonies*, and of course her famous ballad *Time After Time*.

Time After Time is perhaps one of the most frequently covered songs... covered well, covered poorly, covered very, *very* poorly. It has graced showers, karaoke bars, and has been sung in the vehicles by many a solo traveler across this great country time after time, after time. This was a classic and I was fortunate enough to see it LIVE from the creator herself.

The lights dimmed on the set. It was just Cyndi. Just Cyndi and *Time After Time.* I was about to witness greatness.

As she started to sing, it was everything I thought it would be; the performance of a lifetime. A masterpiece...

For about the first seventeen seconds.

And then, then it sounded strangely... *off.* I mean, her timing was all over the place, her wording was backward. It sounded just plain... *weird.*

I thought to myself, and then started yelling at the screen, *Cyndi, you're messing up a song that EVERY-ONE knows! People can tell that you're singing it wrong because they've heard it time after time after time.* Poor Cyndi Lauper. The only hope for the future of Cyndi's career was that not many people watch that show to begin with.

And then it hit me.

She *wrote* the song. She *created* this masterpiece. She was the first. However she sang it was the right way to sing it because when you *are* the original, you earn the right to *never* do it wrong. Several minutes of Ms. Lauper singing and it became clear that I was listening to the most impressive version of *Time After Time* I had ever heard before. Though it was a different than what I knew, it was perfect. It was as *only* Cyndi Lauper could sing it.

In that moment, I knew what I had to do.

The whole problem with my romantic dinner for two was that I was covering someone else's song.... I was "covering" someone else's recipe when what I needed was an *original*.

With my time running slim, I raced to the kitchen, grabbed the rest of the chicken, found some pizza sauce, some canned tomatoes, black olives, and mushrooms. I found some spices in my cupboard that I purchased in college, not because I knew what they were but because they were on sale for 50 cents. I hoped that spices didn't go bad. I took a bag of fancy shredded cheddar out of

the fridge and threw all of it together in the crock-pot
my father had given me when I left home—he knew me
better than I thought. I put the crock-pot on high and
took three steps back.

I had done it. I was creating a masterpiece. I would call
it:

Chicken à la Kindra

And however it turned out, it would be right. It had more
chance of success simply because it was an original. I
stood there in the kitchen of my one-bedroom apartment
and I celebrated for a moment. I was victorious.

And then I had to get ready for a date that just didn't
seem to matter that much anymore.

BE A
STRANGER

It was a Saturday morning in December of 2005. I had been living in Arizona for about two and a half months and had had enough. Work wasn't what I was hoping it would be, I hadn't met any people I particularly cared for, and the *one* person I *did* meet who I *thought* I cared for, turned out to have a live-in girlfriend (and all that time I thought he only wanted to hang out at my place because of my awesome futon).

Yes, two and a half months were enough for me.

On that Saturday morning in December, I made my decision: I was leaving. I had been out the night before (with the people I didn't particularly care for) and woke up with the kind of headache that would make anyone want to leave town. I decided I was moving to Los Angeles. And though I hadn't been there before, I decided to take that weekend to find an L.A. apartment I could call home—because *anything* would feel more like home than Arizona. I packed a bag, grabbed my laptop, and prepared to hit the road.

Just I was about to walk out the door, I passed the mirror that hung on the wall. It was a mirror I bought at IKEA the day I moved to Arizona, not because I needed it or could afford it, but because I loved it.

Actually, I loved what I *saw* when I looked *into* it. The day I purchased that mirror, I had seen hope and excitement in the face that was reflected back to me; the face of someone at the beginning of a great adventure.

However, the face in the mirror on that Saturday morning in December two and a half months later did *not* look hopeful; it was ragged, worn and tired. The hair was matted and the eyes were lonely.

It was not my best day. It was time to leave.

I walked down to my car, in my pajamas more or less,

and drove down the street to the first gas station. I pulled up to a pump and started to fill up. I struggled with the keypad, trying to figure out why it needed *so much* information just to give me a little gas. The handle kept clicking off when I tried to set it on auto-fill. And even before I was done filling up, the machine incessantly asked if I wanted a receipt. I was so anxious to get out of Arizona and so frustrated that the gas station was making it *so* impossible.

And then someone pulled up alongside of me and rolled down his window.

Oh no. I bet my tires are low. Other people were always pointing out that my tires were low.

However, the man behind the wheel said nothing about my tires. Instead he said in a voice that was not wanting or in the least bit suggestive,

"You know, you are really beautiful."

My jaw dropped and my hand slipped from the handle (so the gas immediately stopped pumping). I didn't know what to say. This was the last thing I had ever expected anyone in Arizona to say to me on this particular Saturday, or on *any* Saturday in Arizona.

Thank you? I started to respond... but he just waved, as if it were nothing, and drove off.

I never saw him again.

But I never forgot him.

· · · · ·

Though the phrase "random acts of kindness" has, over the years, become cliché, the recipients of those acts, I believe, have become no less grateful. In a world where friends have to book quality time weeks in advance, where phone calls are replaced with text messages and texts are replaced with tweets, it seems the "stranger" carries a stronger responsibility.

I never moved to California. I was there till Tuesday and then I decided it was time to "come home." When I walked into my apartment after the long drive back, I looked in the mirror that hung on the wall and said to myself, "You know, you are really beautiful."

And in my reflection I saw the hope and excitement begin to return.

THE WINNER'S CREASE

I am a cheater.

I grew up playing board games with my younger brother and sister: CandyLand, Chutes and Ladders, Clue, Battleship, Monopoly, Checkers, Chinese Checkers, and the very obscure but endlessly delightful 13 Dead End Drive.

And every chance I got, I cheated.

I peeked when I wasn't supposed to. I gave myself extra money when I was the banker (and I was *always* the banker). I moved pieces when no one was looking. I even managed to rig the spinner so that it always pointed the direction I wanted. No matter how the deck was shuffled, I always came out on top.

But by far, my favorite cheating strategy was in the Game of LIFE. In LIFE you had to draw cards to determine three major aspects of your LIFE journey: what kind of house you would own, what your job would be and how much money you would make come each payday. In the salary category there was a card for various earning levels: $20,000, $50,000, $80,000, and the biggest salary of all, $100,000.

I was no fool. I knew that in the grand scheme of the game neither the house nor the career mattered. It was all about the money. And while the cards were seemingly impossible to distinguish when face down, I would find a way.

One night shortly after my brother had received LIFE as a gift, I volunteered to pick up all of the cards and pieces and, out of the kindness of my heart, volunteered to put the game away in the toy closet downstairs. Kindness like this was entirely unlike me but nevertheless my younger siblings fell for it. Once alone in the basement, I rummaged through the game until I found the treasured $100,000 Salary Card. I looked over my shoulders to verify that no one was watching and when I confirmed the coast was clear, I took the card and with trained precision *branded it* with a crease. The Winner's Crease. The gloss on the card cracked and the paint separated where the card had been folded. Right through the middle.

This was all by design.

After the card had been branded, I worked to reverse the majority of the damage. I flattened, smoothed, rubbed the card between my hands until it lay *mostly* flat. To the untrained eye the card looked like the result of typical board game wear and tear. Sure, it was a little crinkled. Yeah, there was a little bend in the middle. But it was nothing more than a well-loved component of a family favorite board game.

Well-loved. Yes. It was, after all, $100,000.

I then roughed up each of the other salary cards so it wouldn't look suspicious. And my job was done.

From then on, whenever it was my turn to face the luck-of-the-draw, luck was on my side. Whaddaya know.

Unfortunately, though the days of childhood board games come to an end, the days seem never ending when real life's choices are placed face down in front of us. We know that the right card is in the deck, we just aren't always sure which one it is. More than once I have wished for a way to cheat. To fold down the edge of the direction I should choose next; the direction that will make me a winner. I want to find ways I can cheat, despite learning at a young age that when it comes to *real* LIFE, cheaters never prosper.

• • • • •

It was my junior year of high school.
Yes.
The year of David.

Though our first kiss had been magic, though he had written "love" on a paper bag and given it to me as a gift just days earlier, as mid-February rolled around our relationship desperately needed Cupid's arrow of salvation.

I knew I could win him; I just had to find a way to cheat. I *always* won when I cheated. And then, as if from Aphrodite herself, my opportunity revealed itself.

It was the week before Valentine's Day. For a school fundraiser, the Student Council administered a Find Your True Love compatibility test. It was quite the ordeal. Everyone in the school was given an identity code (for secrecy) and a survey of fifty essential love-match questions. By answering these questions honestly, you could find your perfect match.

The first version of eHarmony.com.

The members of the Student Council visited each classroom to hand out the tests. Each of the questions was to be answered in private and without discussion with or evaluation from other students. The Council members collected the surveys and mailed them off to an unknown destination for tabulation. The survey results arrived on Valentine's Day and for $1 you could purchase your results to discover who your Top 10 True Love Matches were.

And there it was.

My $100,000 card.

I was *on* the Student Council.

I could arrange to be the one to *administer* the tests.

And I did.

When David turned his in to me, even though it had

an anonymous code to protect his identity, I secretly branded it with the Winner's Crease and walked away.

Later that afternoon, I pulled the creased survey out from the stack. I then filled out a questionnaire for myself with David's answers as a reference. Certainly there were a few questions I had to answer differently than he did, such as "Would you rather A) Play sports or B) Be on the speech team?" But overall, I thought my answers naturally matched David's pretty well. I could prefer fishing to sunbathing. My perfect first date could involve video games and be candle-less. I answered as honestly and truthfully as I could and still answer the same as David.

I took note of my anonymous code, shoved my survey in with the rest, and handed them in, pleased that my task was complete. I was pretty certain I would at least be in David's top three and then he would have no choice but to love me. It was science. (And he loved science. And according to the survey, so did I).

One week passed.

It was lunch hour on Valentine's Day and the cafeteria was pure chaos. Kids yelling across the room, groans of disgust and horror, cliques tightly knit together in full gossip mode. Those who had remembered their one dollar bills were racing to the front of the room to get their results. Those who had forgotten their one dollar bills were begging the others. Everyone HAD to know who their top ten True Love matches were.

I knew the time had finally come.

As I made my way to the results table, I overheard disappointment from many of the people I passed:

"My top match is only 19 percent?! That's crap."
"How come none of my people match more than 15 percent? You can't start a future on 15 percent."
"Who is Paul McCartney?"

As it turned out, 21 percent compatibility was about the highest percentage in the entire school (and unfortunately that was between a brother and sister). With such simple questions and such a non-diverse crowd (small town Minnesota high school) it was difficult to determine what algorithm the computing program could have used to deem us all so incompatible. It was kind of a Valentine's Day downer.
For all but one.

One happy sixteen-year-old girl.

One happy girl who was madly in love and now had the paperwork to prove it was justified.

Me.

According to the meticulously developed, scientifically based questionnaire (that only cost a dollar) I was 92 percent compatible with David and he was 92 percent Meant. For. Me. Prom would only be the beginning of our beautiful life together. I had won once again. I was the *best* at these kinds of games.

Then I saw David.

He was furious.

None of his friends had matches higher than 18 percent. None of his friends even *recognized* the names on their lists. None of his friends could believe that *we* were 92 percent compatible. And neither could he. His next closest match was a girl on the volleyball team named Jenny who never talked to people, at 16 percent. He wasn't exactly sure how, but he knew I had cheated. When I tried to protest, tried to defend my honor, tried to explain that I'm not the kind of girl who cheats, he ripped up his compatibility test right there in front of me and walked away.

I stood at the top of the stairs of the cafeteria and watched his blonde hair disappear into the crowd. I was devastated. I knew it was over. (And it was... until a week later when we got back together for another week). It was there, looking down on a sea of incompatible teenagers, I vowed to never use The Winner's Crease again.

• • • • •

I am a recovering cheater. I have left my tactics and schemes behind me. Over the years I have learned to enjoy winning when it happens, but more important to enjoy the twists and turns of fate as the game is played. True not only in board games and compatibility tests, but for all things. After all, it is not the cards I draw that determine whether I win or lose, it is what I *do* with the cards that matters.

BEWARE
THE BUICKS

It was a Friday morning. A *great* morning. The kind of morning they were singing about in the musical *Oklahoma* when they said "Oh what a beautiful morning." The kind of morning you were *born* to live.

I credit gratitude. I was *so* grateful that Friday morning.

I was grateful for my health, I was grateful for my mind, I was grateful for my mom and dad, and all my friends. I was grateful for the great parking spot in the busy Starbucks lot. I was grateful for the inspirational song that was blaring from my car stereo and for the fact that I sound *so good* when I sing in my car alone. I was grateful for the kids in the crosswalk, holding hands, walking to high school, not at all aware of the fact that they were holding up traffic.

I was completely overcome, *smitten*, with gratitude. Nothing could bring me down.

Then, I had to make a left turn. It was a particularly tricky spot for a left turn because the traffic from the east comes pretty quick around a curve, leaving little time to react. From the west there are a lot of opportunities for cars to pull out of parking lots, breaking up the openings when traffic is stopped at the light.

I waited, patiently creeping a little bit further out so as to maximize my opportunity when it arose. Moments later, as if the universe had ordered it just for me, the stoplight turned red to the west and the road was empty to the east. I started to pull out, *grateful* to be claiming my place on the road, when I noticed out of the corner of my eye a spotless, white Buick screech out of one of the many parking lots between the stoplight and me.

In most cases, I would have gone anyway. The parking lot entrance was far enough away. However, the spotless, white Buick had pulled out with such force, such speed, I was certain it would smash into the side of my car. At that speed, I didn't want to risk it.

Besides, it had to be a gang member, robber, or thief driving that vehicle. Only maniacs drove that fast.

Then.
As if ordered by the universe.
In the same instant I decided *not* to pull forward, the spotless, white Buick slowed to a crawl. An *"I'm crawling across the desert and haven't had any water in three days and I'm about to pass out or hallucinate"* type of crawl.

Dammit.

I could feel the gratitude drain from my body. Then, as the spotless, white Buick passed I caught a glimpse of the driver.

A little old lady.

A little old lady straining her neck to see over the steering wheel, curlers still in her hair. Behind her, from the west, was a stream of traffic three miles long, and from the east cars came around the curve like horses on a race track.

I. Was. *So. Mad.*

Why did she have to pull out then? Why couldn't she
have used her lead foot until she drove *past* me? I
should have called the cops to have her arrested for
reckless driving; she was probably going eighty-five
when she pulled out. Buicks go from zero to eighty-five
in point-five seconds, right?

I sat at that intersection for no fewer than ten minutes
(or so it felt), as I stewed in my own fury. And in those
gratitude-less moments, I felt like a child who got a balloon at the bank and as I walked out to the parking lot
holding that balloon, I got distracted—my mom called
my name, or my sister pushed me—and the balloon
slipped from my fingers and danced away across the sky
and all I can do is stare and know it is gone.

I have felt this way with Gratitude at times. It takes only
a small distraction and it's gone.

But I am not a child. And I am certainly helpless in
those moments when gratitude escapes me. Every
moment of gratitude lost, a moment of greatness is
wasted; therefore, to handle these lapses in gratitude a
little better, I try to come prepared. For me, preparation

means this:

• • • • •

I decided to take a trip, to travel back to a memory. In a moment's time I was standing outside the San Diego Airport. It was July 2006. The sun was hot, and I could smell the ocean. I had never been to San Diego before but this trip was special for a different reason; I was going to see Michael.

Michael was a man I had met at work. I knew within a day or two we were destined to be together so I began dropping subtle hints, then less subtle, until finally I would stand in his office doorway, ask him about the status of a purchase order and then ask when we could start dating. Risky? Yes. But it kind of worked. After several months of trying to convince him to fall in love with me, followed by the best first kiss in the history of all mankind, he had invited me to come visit him in California where he lived part time.

At the time of his invitation, I wasn't sure *what* we were. Sure he had kissed me, but were we dating? Exclusive? Friends? Just Coworkers with some west coast task? These questions hung with the beachy humidity as I stood outside Arrivals in a green dress from Target,

strappy sandals, big sunglasses and my blonde hair
shifting nervously in the breeze.

My heart rattled with excitement as Michael pulled up in
a gold, 1987 Volvo—his beach-mobile.

As I threw my luggage in the back and climbed in,
Michael smiled at me.
I had never been to Southern California before, but I
knew with that smile it was the greatest place on Earth.
Michael told me we were going to Coronado Island—his
hometown.
I was so nervous I tried not to talk; when in doubt, don't.
say. anything.

The drive from the airport was beautiful as it wound
through downtown. The streets were packed with people
erasing their troubles with ocean air. Soon we neared
the bridge to cross the bay. I rolled down the window.
The wind was wild as we climbed above the water on our
way to paradise.

It was *then* that Michael reached across the console for
my hand.
When he touched it, I knew I was done.

In that moment, with the sun, the sea, the city, and Michael—the man who would ask me to marry him a few years later—I felt gratitude so intense I couldn't breathe.

• • • • •

Sitting at the intersection that Friday morning, fuming, I recalled my first trip over the Coronado Bridge and the first time my dear husband held my hand. All it took was that memory and I was right back where I needed to be.

Grateful.

Seconds later, I turned left and continued down the road.

"Oh what a beautiful morning, oh what a beautiful day. I've got a beautiful feeling, everything's going my way."

WHAT IT TAKES TO RUN A MARATHON

Every few months or so I decide I am going to run a marathon. I believe that if I run a marathon I will be a "Runner." A Runner is something I never thought I would be, and to become one... well, that would be a *very* big deal.

Once I make this decision, I begin the planning. Marathon running takes *a lot* of planning. First, you have to decide *which* marathon you are going to run. I typically choose the Phoenix Rock 'n' Roll Marathon in January. Every January.

After you choose the marathon, you then have to decide which training program you're going to use.

Marathons take *a lot* of training. My favorite training program involves a lot of structure, a lot of very specific instructions. Structure is good for a runner: Monday, rest; Tuesday, run "X" miles; Wednesday, run "X" miles; Thursday, run "X" miles; Friday, rest; Saturday, run way farther than you thought you could; Sunday, cross-train.

After I familiarize myself with the schedule, I then fill it in on my desk calendar. I write down on each particular day how many miles I'm supposed to run. This way, I will not be confused—I can simply look at my calendar and know how far I should go. Unfortunately, I often mess up, skip a week somehow, and have to erase three weeks' worth and start over. It is a very time-consuming task, but necessary if you wish to successfully run a marathon.

Also necessary is entering the *same* information in the calendar on my phone; this way I can know the miles I need to run no matter where I am. I'll admit, this is more tedious than the desk calendar process, but a runner's got to know how far they're supposed to run on what days, even if they're not sitting at their desk, staring at their calendar.

You might ask, Well can't "a Runner" just go out and start running around however far they choose on any given day just for the simple fact that they love running?

The answer is no.

The next step is to prepare my iPod. Everyone needs a strong, motivating playlist to get through the long runs and to make the short runs enjoyable. I have two iPods. A Shuffle and a Nano. The Shuffle is limited in its abilities. The Nano I stole from Michael and only works when it wants. Sadly, my run-tracking device (you should get one of those too) doesn't work with the Shuffle so therefore I run with both. The Shuffle and the Nano. BOTH iPods need to be well-equipped with songs-for-running. But not the same songs. I wouldn't want to take my earphones out of the Nano when it dies only to hear the same songs again when I plug into the Shuffle. So, two strong, motivating playlists are necessary to run a marathon.

Then it is time for the running apparel. Shoes designed for my feet. Socks that don't slide or soak. Shorts that are comfy and cute. Tops that support with style. Accessories that keep wild hair tamed. I'm telling you, running a marathon is a lot of work.

Next... well, I have to be honest; I haven't really made it past that point. While I spend all my time preparing, preparing to *start taking steps* to run, I have never actually moved my feet in a running motion.

• • • • •

I was at an awkward time.

An awkward time with my stories, with my writing, with my telling and I just wasn't sure what to do next. I spent much of my time Googling "ways to make money writing," or "so you want to be a writer and earn some money" or "different places to tell stories" or "so you want to tell stories and earn some money." I made lists in a notebook of various people who did various things with writing or speaking or storytelling. I carried the notebook around with me, like a security blanket, convinced that, just by holding it, I was making progress.

In an effort to find some validation, I reached out to a writer-friend living in New York City who was happy to help. In one particular email communication, my writer-friend pointed out an area where I could improve—an area where I was getting in my own way. I agreed and responded:

"Guess it's time to start taking the steps to do it..."

To which my New York City friend (in true New York City fashion) responded:

"I love that you are so adorable that you say 'time to start taking the steps to do it.' Sh*t, girl, you kill me. I literally sit at my computer laughing my a** off, but I know you are serious. So I don't tell you. But really, it is adorable and I know this is offensive, so PLEASE, allow me this offense, but… Wow. 'Time to START taking the STEPS to do it.' So that would mean what, exactly? Hahahaha. I love it. Here's Harlem talkin': 'Just do it.'"

Hmm.

When I read the response, I was a little mad and totally annoyed.
I mean, *come on.*
Just do it? That's not Harlem talking, that's Nike.
And *laughing* at me? What kind of writer-friend does *that*? Wasn't it obvious that there were steps that needed to be taken before really getting into it?

And then a thought occurred to me.
I told my first story in fifth grade. I was eleven and I knew *that day* that I was on to something. Twenty years later and I was *still* preparing to "start taking steps."

My friend was right. It was laughable.

And I do it all the time. Whether it is running or writing or dieting or whatever, regardless of which "race" I am hoping to complete, I am a faux-marathoner. I am always *preparing* to *start* taking steps, when in reality, there are. no. steps. in between doing it and not.

• • • • •

Will I ever *actually* run a marathon? I'm not sure. Honestly, I don't really like running that much. However, actual-marathon or not, I have resolved to stop "taking steps" and calling it progress. From now on, following the advice from Harlem (or Nike), I will just do it.

THE
LIGHT BOX

Someone once told me that October is the reason people move to Arizona. It's true. Though the change in season isn't as dramatic as leaves turning from green to gold, there is something irresistible about the relief of an Arizona October; when the oppressive heat of the summer has lifted and only a comfortable warmth remains.

It was on one particularly flawless October morning that I decided to take a stroll through the grassy lawns of an urban Arizona park. I put on my shorts and tank, grabbed a coffee, and set out to enjoy the natural outdoor beauty.

However, on this walk, I experienced a different beauty...

As I came around the corner of some well trimmed hedges and headed toward the fountain where water defied gravity, something unusual caught my eye. I stopped.

Positioned around this particular area of the park were forty-three large light boxes standing six and a half feet tall and five feet wide. Each light box had text that was arranged to look just like a vision chart at the eye doctor; the one with a big "E" at the top followed by rows of increasingly smaller (and virtually impossible to read) letters below. Except there weren't *letters* on these boxes, but instead a collection of words. The top word was large and ominous and followed by rows of increasingly smaller words.

It was striking. In a city where desert-scapes are considered fine art, I was surprised to see something so modern.

Of course, I had no idea what it meant.
Fortunately, the display came with a short description (I appreciate abstract art *more* when there is a guide to the abstractness), and I learned very quickly that this was more than art; it was history. It was future.

Each one of the light boxes represented a president of the United States. Research was gathered at the University of California, Santa Barbara for the American Presidency Project. The researchers analyzed the State of the Union addresses of the individual presidents and determined which unique word each one used most. Then an artist brought the research to life using the forty-three light boxes. The large letter "E" typically seen at the top of a vision test was replaced with the word used most by each president during his annual addresses:

George Washington—GENTLEMEN
James Buchanan (right before Lincoln)—SLAVERY
Abraham Lincoln—EMANCIPATION
Lyndon B Johnson—TONIGHT (it was the first State of the Union to be televised so the immediacy of the message was exciting)
Nixon—TRULY
Ronald Reagan—DEFICITS
Bill Clinton—21ST (as we prepared for a new century)
George W. Bush—TERROR

Walking around the exhibit it was... eerie; like taking a walk through history, one word at a time. I hadn't thought much about our early presidents since Mr. Arnold's seventh grade history class (and even then my attention was minimal), yet *I* could, in many cases, identify each president simply by reading one word from a distance of fifty feet. The word at the top of each box, in most cases, entirely defined the term in office—as if they were simply themes rather than results of careful algorithms to determine frequency of use. One word. I was completely captivated. I couldn't look away. And then I started thinking....

What if someone were to distill me down?
What if someone were to take the words I used the most, in a year, in a decade, in a day.
What words would dominate my light box?
What words would define *me*?
In a glance, what would someone know of my life, my mission?

Every day we have choices in the words we use and, for better or worse, our words define us to the world. They are an expression of our attitude, and attitude can make or break a person. Many talented people have never lived up to who they could've or should've been for no other reason than their negative attitude; a demise fueled by the many negative words they chose to share. If ever we wonder what is holding us back, what is keeping us from greatness, all we have to do is listen closely to the words we choose.

I walked away from that exhibit, and over the next couple October days I pondered the light boxes. After a week, I was ready to go back, to look at them again. I felt better prepared for what I might learn about myself. However, when I returned to the park where the light boxes had been... they were gone. Like a mirage in the desert, they left not a trace.

I stood there, my sneakers on the sidewalk, my hands in the pockets of my sleeveless vest, quiet for a moment. Then I turned, and on that perfect Arizona October morning, walked home hoping that, should someday someone create a light box for me, the word at the top would make me proud.

A PLACE
TO BECOME

I have not an athletic bone in my body.

The first clear memory of my staggering inability to do *anything* requiring flexibility, strength, or agility was during First Grade Physical Fitness Testing. I *hated* Physical Fitness Testing. I hated the Shuttle Run. I hated the endurance walk/run (which I always turned into a leisurely stroll). And though it *sounds* easy, I could never do the V-Sit and Reach. However, towering above ALLLL my other hatreds, my most despised event: the pull-ups. The pull-ups are to blame for killing a tiny portion of my little first grade soul.

The test took place out on the playground. On a fall

morning as gray as the hair of our old lady gym teacher, we stood, huddled and single file beneath the dreaded uneven bars that hung over a pit of small rocks and gravel. I was last in line. Partially because I had just moved to the school district and didn't know anyone, partially because it was my strategy; I thought there was a chance—*a chance*—that the teacher might die before it was my turn. The old gray-haired teacher was beside the bars-of-torture, clipboard in hand, face as cold as the metal folding chair upon which she sat. One by one the first graders approached the bar. One by one they raised their hands toward the bar and jumped to grasp it. One by one the old teacher counted out loud the pull-ups each child completed. She then wrote the number down—no doubt to someday pass it on to the attendant at the Pearly Gates.

Derek: 10
Jaci: 7
Marianne: 4

Soon the kids in line started to count along with her. Shouting with each chin-to-bar ONE! TWO! THREE! They sometimes got a little carried away with the *shout-ing* and focused less on the *counting*, therefore getting a little ahead of the *actual* number of pull-ups each child completed. This inevitably led to a shouting match between twenty-five first graders and one gray lady gym teacher who was trying to keep the count accurate; heaven forbid she give away a freebie.

Curt: NINE! TEN!! ELEVEN!!
Evan: FOURTEEN!! FIFTEEN!! SIXTEEN!!
Angela: ONE! TWO!!

After Angela, I had no choice. It was my turn, and as far as I could tell, the teacher still had a pulse. *"Maybe it won't be so bad,"* I thought. *"Even Angela Ferguson was able to pull off two pull-ups and she flailed her arms like she was swimming when she ran."*

I approached the bar hoping that the sudden fall breeze was an indication of the shifting of the winds of my athletic existence. *I could do this.* I ran my hands down my dress to make sure the patterns of pink elephants and yellow monkeys were smooth and situated. If all else failed, at least I would look put-together.

I raised my hands in the air and jumped to grab the bar like the other kids had. I failed. I tried again. Failed. The kids started counting:

ONE!! TWO!! THREE!! for the number of times I jumped
and missed the bar.

This was not good.

Finally the old gray lady gym teacher put down her
clipboard, grabbed me at my elephant-monkey-printed
waist, and hoisted me up to the bar. I felt my hands
grip like tiny steel traps around it. The teacher sat back
down and I started to Pull. Up.

The next few seconds were the longest of my childhood.

I pulled. I pulled. I didn't move. I kicked my legs. I
strained my neck. I grunted. I looked to the bar and
wondered when my arms had gotten SO LONG that the
bar was a mile away. I looked past the bar to the heav-
ens, but they offered me no comfort. I pulled. I pulled.
I kicked my legs. All the while I heard the kids behind
me in less-than-perfect unison s u s p e n d i n g the
word *ONE* as long as possible. It was so long it started to
sound like slow monastery chanting.

OOOONNNNEEEE

I. was. desperate-mortified-humiliated-spent. By this

point I had been hanging from the bar for no fewer than fifteen minutes. That *had* to count for *something*. I made one final attempt. With a sudden gust of that fall breeze at my back, I squeeeeeezed my little first-grade butt cheeks as hard as I could, *willing* them to propel my chin to the bar.

Just once. Just one time.

But alas, all that did was cause my bottom to seize up in a fit of pain and fury while the breeze lifted my dress up over my face, blinding me in a sea of printed fabric. I fell to the pit of small rocks and gravel below. My pink elephant-yellow monkey dress lay disgraced in a crumpled heap around me as I writhed on the ground. It was only between sobs that I heard the sound of first-grade voices yelling in unison—only this time it wasn't endearing celebratory counting. No, this sounded more like the musical-mechanical laughter of a small-town carnival ride. Eerie. Frightening. I pushed the hair from my eyes, and with small rocks and gravel stuck to my face I looked to my classmates who were shouting: *I see London, I see France, I see Kindra's underpants!*

It was not a good day. It was not a good couple days. I was sore for a week. My ego was sore for much longer.

I have never questioned the fact that I do not have an athletic bone in my body, but that hasn't stopped me from wishing.... Since that cloudy day, over a pit of small rocks and gravel, I have always wished it could be different. I have wished to *become*; to become the person with the strength, the heart of an athlete.

To become *more*.

• • • • •

Michael and I got married on April 4, 2009.

I ate nothing but vegetables and lentils for a full three weeks before.

I. Looked. Amazing.

Then, on my honeymoon, I ate *everything*. Any time of day, anywhere we went, anything I could get my hands on. Though there was fresh fish and island fruit a-plenty, I opted for anything fried, starchy, and chocolate. While other honeymooners were making love, I was eating a bag of Cheetos an hour. Why not? I was married!

When we got back home, I couldn't fit into my wedding dress.

For some people this transition takes five years. For me, it was a week. I decided it was perhaps *not* the best strategy to "let myself go" so early, so when my friend Kathleen mentioned taking a spin class with her, I considered going.

I *also* considered *not* going. I had been to a spin class once before at my local gym about three years earlier. Once. And even though the instructor was *almost* old enough to be my grandmother, it was the worst hour of my life. I vowed never to spin again.

But Kathleen insisted this wasn't like other spin classes and visions of my wedding dress haunted me, so reluctantly I agreed. We planned to meet at the spin studio a little before class started at 5:30.
I thought she meant 5:30 *p.m.*
She did not.
She meant 5:30 in the *morning.* She meant when it was *still dark* outside.
"I do not wake up when it is dark," I told Kathleen. In fact, I rarely climbed out of bed before 8 a.m., which gave me just enough time to rinse, ponytail, mascara, find clothes that were mostly unwrinkled and bolt out the door to work in an attempt to make it there by nine.

Nevertheless, my desire to be desired was (only slightly) stronger than my desire to sleep, so on a Thursday morning in late April I rolled myself out of bed, into the car, and to the spin class—all the while trying *not* to wake up. I arrived, paid five dollars for my first class, and walked from the lobby into the studio.

It was pitch black. The floors were black, the ceilings were black, the walls were black. Hanging in the four corners of the room were massive (black) speakers that were already playing music that sounded like what might be played in the dungeon of a castle. There were floor-to-ceiling mirrors on three of the black walls, creating the illusion of endless rows of bikes. Fifty in all. Fifty metal frames. Fifty heavy steel wheels. They looked like robot dinosaur carcasses lined up in three rows on the floor, and one elevated row in the back. In the center front of the room, sitting atop a two-foot platform, was the Head Bike. It glowed while flameless candles flickered beneath—not unlike a séance.

I was about to climb onto one of the menacing pieces of machinery when Kathleen stopped me and told me I must put on a tattered, stinky pair of special spin shoes to snap into the pedals. Feet Cuffs, I called them. Tennis shoes were not allowed—they made escaping too easy.

Shortly after, I was a spin prisoner and it was only after I was thoroughly trapped that I realized my bike seat was positioned too low. I turned to Kathleen, who had snapped into the bike next to me, and shared my concern. "Oh no," she said in a no-big-deal tone. "The seat doesn't matter.... We don't sit down."

To clarify: Yes. They stand the whole time. Yes. The class is an hour.

As other riders filed into the studio, Kathleen gave me a quick (survival) lesson.

"The goal is to always ride on the beat; to snap your right foot to the bottom of the stroke on every drumbeat. If the song has a slow beat, the ride is slow. If the song has a fast beat, the ride is fast. If the song has a beat that hits 125 times in a minute, we simply *fly*; perfectly synched, beautifully choreographed." She made it sound so easy.... Just then the instructor walked in. Kathleen leaned over again and whispered in wonder and amazement. "Don't worry. You'll want to spin every day for the rest of your life when you see what her body looks like." The instructor, Goddess of All Spinners, cuffed herself into the head bike and immediately removed her tank top (apparently riding mostly naked was normal at this studio) and I gasped.

Yes. I would spin every day for the rest of my life if I could look like that.

Kathleen shouted to the Goddess, "Oooh! Oooh! I brought a friend!"

Susie, the instructor, Goddess of All Spinners, turned to face us. There was an uncanny resemblance to celebrity personal trainer Jillian Michaels, except I feared that Susie was stronger, and a little bit meaner. "Some friend *you* are," she threatened in the microphone from the top of her pedestal. "This is the hardest class all week."

It was true. Susie was known for bringing grown, athletic men to their knees in a puddle of their own sweat and vomit.

I considered running but the music started.
I had no choice.
Especially since I couldn't get my feet out of the pedals.

And so began my *second*-ever spin class. I'm not going to say it was pretty. I'm not going to say it was fun. My socks were soaked, my hair was dripping, my towel was drenched, my heart felt as though it might explode and I was barely through the warm up. I watched the athlete spinners in the front row from my bike in the back of the room. I watched their feet go around in circles at 125 beats per minute for ten minutes straight. I listened to them shout and howl as the music reached its crescendo, as the instructor flipped on black lights that made the whole room glow. I heard them push each other, cheer each other on. I watched them move with the music. And I was overcome.

Never, not since that pull-up test, had I wanted to be an athlete so badly.

I made it to the end of the class. As people started to file out I saw the Goddess look my way and say, into the microphone:

"Hey 'Friend,' " you're still here. That's pretty good."

I stopped.
She was right.
I was still there.
And if I could do it once.
I could do it again.

At 6:45 a.m. that morning, after wringing out every item of clothing on my body and a quart of water from my hair, I decided to make a few purchases:

Twelve Spin Classes. $96.00

One pair of Feet Cuffs. $120.00

The first steps on the path to becoming something you never thought you could.... Priceless.

And at 5:30 a.m. the next morning, I was there.

Every morning I watched the spinners in the front row. I came when they came and I did what they did. On days when I wanted to sleep, I spun. On days when I wanted to snuggle, I spun. On days when it was too cold or too hot or too dark, I spun. I pushed myself, I dared myself, and when I doubted if I belonged, I reminded myself that none of those spinners had been there the day of First Grade Pull-Ups. None of them knew I wasn't an athlete.

Several months later, on a fall morning as gray as the hair of my old lady gym teacher, I went to the spin studio. It was on that day that Susie, Goddess of All Spinners, invited me to sit on the bike next to hers in the front row. She wasn't instructing the class. No, someone else was doing that. However, it was clear she was instructing *me*. We sat, side by side, in our sports bras and as the class progressed and the music for the fastest song of the morning started, Susie leaned over and said, "I'll tell you when you can take a break. Don't break until I tell you."

I silently nodded (and cried a little inside).

The music played at 125 beats per minute. My feet flew in circles, my right foot striking the bottom of the rotation every time the drum sounded. Two minutes in I wiped my forehead with the white towel that was glowing in the black light, all the while not missing a beat.

At four minutes, I glanced at Susie. She was staring down at her handlebars, and though it was dark, I could tell in her expression she was saying "I didn't tell you to take a break, did I?"
She scared me. I kept going.

Seven minutes in, I started counting in my head the number of times my foot hit the drum. ONE!! TWO!! THREE!! Anything to distract me. Anything to keep me sane. Anything to stop the sneaking suspicion that I couldn't do it.

Eight minutes in the instructor yelled, "Advanced spinners—you've got two minutes left." Susie, still staring at her handlebars, still spinning, said "You've got this."

At the ten-minute mark, the music ended, we slowed our feet, and the Goddess of All Spinners looked at me and smiled. "Now you can take a break."

And I did.

Maybe it was the lack of oxygen to my brain, or perhaps it was the volumes of sweat pouring into my eyes, but as I sat down on my bike seat to catch my breath I felt... *different*. Like a weight had been lifted, or a skeleton had been removed from my closet. No *normal* person could accomplish what I had just done; it was a victory available only to someone with the strength, heart, and determination of an *athlete*. And that athlete was *me*.

There, in the darkness and the quiet between songs, I closed my eyes for a moment.
I finally let go of the little girl who couldn't pull her chin above the bar.
And I knew she would be pleased with what I'd become.

THE FALL OF MY FRESHMAN YEAR

It was the fall of my freshman year of high school.

Sometimes still, when the night is clear, the air crisp and scented with that undeniable "fall smell," I get a fleeting feeling in my stomach that used to come right before a high school football game. It would be dark, chilly, and absolutely thrilling. There were so many variables, so many different ways the night could turn out. And not a single one had anything to do with football. Would "X" boy look at me? Would "Y" girl be my friend outside of Language Arts class? Would I look cool enough in my marching band outfit? Would I be invited to a friend's house after the game? *Which* friend? Who are my friends?

Ah, the wonders of a teenage mind. All of the questions really boiling down to, Who Am I? Or more important, Who Should I Be? Who do I need to be to have the people I *want* to like me, to like me? What do I need to change? How far am I willing to go?

It was the fall of my freshman year of high school in the small Minnesota town where I grew up. Claire was one of my few friends who had survived the inevitable friend shuffle that happens the summer between eighth and ninth grade. She was taller than me with auburn curls, perfectly placed freckles, and ice-blue eyes. She had the luxury of "early female development"—something I envied, something she was still getting used to (and was certainly not convinced it was a luxury at all). Though we were the same age, Claire seemed much more worldly than me. She had older sisters who shared their wisdom, and since I was the oldest in my family, she was generous to pass those findings on to me. She was the first person to introduce me to music beyond church and musical theater. She was also the first person I ever knew to like a boy old enough to drink alcohol and who lived in *Minneapolis*, a place not so far in distance, but worlds away from our sleepy little hometown.

That fall semester, Claire and I spent many a lunch

hour discussing how she could make Mr. Minneapolis like her. We started with fixing her hair differently. That didn't work. We tried doing her makeup differently, to look more grown up. That didn't work. One afternoon she suggested wearing clothes that showed more legs, more boobs. I protested. Perhaps because I didn't have any boobs. Perhaps because boobs in general still kind of scared me. Perhaps it was because it sounded like something I had seen Samantha do on *Who's the Boss?* and it didn't end well. Whatever the reason, it didn't matter; Claire was determined. When that still didn't work, she decided that she would drink alcohol with him, that maybe if she were drunk, he would like her. Despite my arguing against it, while *I* was sitting at the high school football game, holding my frozen flute in my mittened hand, *she* was in a dimly lit Minneapolis apartment drinking with men who should have known better, as she desperately tried to be who she thought they wanted.

Finally, one Friday afternoon, she came to me. Her auburn hair hanging in curls that only nature could create, her freckles perfectly placed and her ice-blue eyes resolute. She spoke with a determined tone. She knew what she had to do.

She would have sex with him.

My jaw dropped. I'll admit I barely knew what sex was. I mean, I *thought* I knew, but I didn't really know until many years later (and really, it's still up for debate). I *did* know, however, that this was *not* the solution. Even though she was "worldly" I knew Claire was still a girl, just like me.

"Claire, this is a big decision. A decision that once you make it, you can never change back. You can never change back to the Claire you are now."

She looked at me and said, "I don't want to *be* the Claire I am now."

That Friday night, I went to the high school varsity football game, while Claire went to downtown Minneapolis. At the game, the quarterback of the freshman team told me (behind the bleachers, while I held a cup of hot chocolate, after I had changed out of my marching band uniform), that he liked *someone.* He liked a girl, and her name started with a *K*....

I'll admit, I didn't think much about Claire the rest of the night.

· · · · ·

Looking back years later on that fall of my freshman year, I remembered a story I once read, an old Egyptian tale. *The Black Prince.* And though I don't recall the exact wording, the message haunted me. Here is the story as I remember it.

———————————

There once was a young man who lived in a small village that was part of a large empire, in the deserts of Egypt. This young man was ugly, lazy, and for all intents and purposes, worthless to the outside world, though his heart was pure and his intentions always well meaning. All he did all day long was play his flute and wander around. Finally, in the late afternoon sun, he would become tired from all the wandering and flute playing, and he would lay down (wherever) and sleep. His mother was certain this boy would one day fall asleep beside the river, roll in, and drown.

One day, he came across a white stone wall that he had never seen before. He scaled the wall and as he reached the top, he looked into the most beautiful garden oasis he had ever seen. A stream ran between tall, vibrant palms and blooming flowers as it glistened like diamonds in the desert sun. However, despite all of this beauty, the young man could not draw his eyes away from a most mesmerizing sight. At the end of the stream was a crystal-blue pond, and beside the pond sat the most exquisite young woman this young man had ever seen. Her hair hung long and curled and dark down her back. Her face was delicate but strong. Her lips were soft and the same color as the flowing pink fabric of her gown. And her eyes were alive with the mysteries of the night. The young man watched as she sat dreamily by the water's edge. He did not know what to say, he did not know how to reach out to her. So instead of using words, he played his flute from atop that white stone wall. Day after day the young man returned. Day after day he played his music; music that flowed from his soul, the music of love. He never saw her look up. He never saw her see him, and still, he played on....

One day, as he wandered through the village, he heard others speaking of a beautiful girl who was said to enjoy the most beautiful garden in all of Egypt. As the young man listened more closely, he knew that his love and the girl of whom they spoke must be one and the same. He also learned, to his great dismay, that this young woman was none other than the Pharaoh's daughter. The young man was devastated. He knew that no matter how many silly songs, no matter how many days he climbed that white stone wall, he would never have her. He was just an ugly, lazy, worthless man. However, the same gossiping villagers had another story to tell, that of a magical man who lived in the desert. A man who had the power to transform a person... to change their soul, to change their destiny. The young man demanded to know exactly how to find this magical man. The villagers told him to travel three days and three nights into the desert. There, in an impossible oasis, he would find his magical man.

With that the young man turned and walked into the desert.

For three days and three nights he wandered, playing his flute as he walked. Finally he came to an impossible oasis and there, on the edge of a watering hole, stood the magical man. The young man told his story. He begged to be changed to a warrior, a hero, a fierce and powerful man. He begged to become a prince the Pharaoh's daughter would love. The magical man took pause, looking at this young man who didn't appear to be ugly, lazy, *or* worthless. He warned,

"Young man, this is a big decision. A decision that once

you make it, you can never change back. You can never change back to the man you are now."

The young man looked at him and said, "I don't want to be the man I am now."

Days and weeks passed. The young man's mother, after waiting endlessly for her son to return, assumed he had finally fallen in the river and drowned. She held a funeral in his honor. Egypt was also suffering. Bits and pieces were being conquered and taken by surrounding empires. Despite the efforts of the Pharaoh's men, nothing seemed to help.

Then one day, from the depths of the desert, walked a man. This man was impossibly handsome. Charming, strong, and dressed entirely in black. He asked to see the Pharaoh, his voice so powerful the soldiers took him straight away. The Black Prince told the Pharaoh that he could change the fate of his empire, take back the territories that had been lost. The Pharaoh agreed and within weeks, the Black Prince had accomplished all that he said he would.

The Pharaoh threw a celebration throughout the entire land in honor of the bravery and wisdom of the Black

Prince. All of Egypt attended. At the end of the evening the Black Prince was called to the throne where the Pharaoh stood; his daughter, the most beautiful woman in all of Egypt, standing beside him. The Pharaoh announced that as a reward, the Black Prince was to marry the Pharaoh's daughter.

As the first smile spread across the face of the man who was now the Black Prince, the Pharaoh's daughter stepped forward. Her hair hung long, black, and curled down her back. Her face was delicate, and colorless. And her eyes were empty. She spoke to her father.

"Father, if it is your will, I will marry this man. But I will tell you, that I can never love him. You see, I gave my heart away to a young man long ago. A man who used to climb the white wall of my garden and play the music of my soul with his flute. I don't know that he ever saw me; I don't know that he ever knew I was there, but I loved him Father. Then one day, he stopped coming. I sent all of my servants, all of my handmaidens to find him only to learn that he had drowned in the river. I attended the funeral in his honor. So though I will marry whomever you wish, I will never know love like that again for my heart drowned with him."
All of Egypt was silent.

The Black Prince looked at the woman who stood before him, and in her empty eyes he could see the reflection of the young man he used to be. He watched as the reflection handed over his hand-carved flute to the magical man in the desert; a payment in exchange for the man he was today. It was as if he could faintly hear the words of warning, "you can never change back...."

It was then the Black Price spoke.

"I have had a love like yours once. I too, have lost that love. For this, I cannot ask you to marry me."

Without another word, the Black Prince turned and walked into the desert, never to be seen again.

———————————————

I didn't hear from Claire that entire weekend. Monday morning at school I found her at her locker. Same hair, same freckles, but her ice-blue eyes looked strangely cold. I asked what had happened... if she had gone through with her plan.

"Yes," was all she really said.

Though there were no princes, or Pharaoh's daughters,

or magical men, I imagine that Claire felt the same way that young man did when he fully understood the meaning of "… you can never change back." Claire and I grew apart over the rest of the semester. I was busy with speech meets and dating high school boys, and at the end of the semester, Claire moved with her family to a different school, a different state.

I remember, on that last day before Christmas break, dressed in her black winter coat, Claire turned and walked out of the school, never to be seen again.

• • • • •

Freshman year seems like a lifetime away. However, sometimes still, when the night is clear, the air crisp and scented with that undeniable "fall smell," I get a fleeting feeling in my stomach that brings me back to the wonders of a teenage mind. Where all of the questions really boil down to, Who am I? Or who should I be? What do I need to change? How far am I willing to go? With time, I have come to the understanding that these questions do not disappear with age or experience. If anything, as the years pass these questions become *more* prevalent and *more* profound, with consequences far more severe.

So as you wander the desert, seeking the magic to make the change you desire, heed the warning and remember: With some decisions, you can never change back to the person you are now.

RAPUNZEL, RAPUNZEL

My hair has always been my thing.

I can't say I always *knew* it was my thing... but it definitely always has been.

As a child my hair hung in heavy, thick, golden brown sheets halfway down my back. It was more or less straight but if it rained I would get a curly halo around my face. I spent endless mornings sitting on the kitchen or living room or bedroom floor with my mother sitting on a chair right behind me, my head held tightly (mercilessly) between her knees. She had a comb and an assortment of rubber bands and bows: her tools of torture. She yanked and parted and pulled. My head would fight, my neck would strain—I think my spine and my skull actually separated from each other.

I would scream and cry and *beg* that she just cut it all off. *Please*, put me out of my misery. And every time she would say, "Kindra, someday you are going to LOVE this hair," or "Kindra, for the rest of your life you are going to hear, 'I wish I had your hair.'"

She was basically saying, "Your hair is your Thing." She was right. I knew for *sure* she was right the last day of fourth grade when I had it all chopped off, started being mistaken for a boy, and my fourth grade boyfriend broke up with me saying, "That's the ugliest thing I've ever seen."

In the face of such brutal honesty, I couldn't help but wonder if my hair was all I had. As many young girls do, I began taking inventory on everything that was wrong with me; my teeth were prisoners behind a steel bar, my legs weren't as skinny as the other girls' legs, my bottom was rounder than the other girls' bottoms, and my clothes were hand-me-downs on the edge of hideous. I was awkward, I was nerdy, I was loud even when I didn't mean to be.

However, despite everything else, I had my hair.

Now, as a grown woman, I understand that, yes, I love my hair, but it doesn't define me. I know there are many things about me that are fabulous, and I try to remind myself of those things regularly. However, despite my grown woman-ness, sometimes the insecurities of my past come back to haunt me.

· · · · ·

It was two days before the 4th of July and I was in sunny Coronado, California, sitting outside Cafe 1134 on Orange Avenue with Michael and my laptop. We had been sitting outside this café for three hours; watching the people and saying hello to friends as they passed. One of Michael's friends pulled up a chair, introduced herself to me, and joined us for a bit. We were casually visiting and at one point she asked me,

"Does your hair naturally curl that way?"

"Oh, no, I use a curling iron. I've gotten pretty good at it over the years."

"It looks really nice."

Now, because I am a grown woman, because I know my hair doesn't define me, because I have left behind the foolish insecurities of my past, my natural response *should* have been: "Thank you." And *stop*.

But instead, *instead*, I started talking about DJ Tanner. DJ Tanner, the eldest daughter on my favorite childhood sitcom, *Full House*.

Sitting there, on a beautiful California afternoon with a woman I had just met, I went on to talk about the episode where DJ Tanner wanted to lose weight for Kimmy's pool party.

"In an effort to look like the models in the magazine," I explained to Michael's friend, whom I had just met, "DJ stopped eating and went to the gym until she fell off the treadmill. Fortunately, Uncle Jesse had an intervention where he asked DJ (with cheesy music playing in the background) to share all of the things she had going for her. The only thing I remember DJ saying was, 'I have *great* hair.' And I totally knew how DJ felt; that's how I feel. I mean, I may not have *everything* going for me—I may not have the best legs, or bottom, or clothes. I might be nerdy and loud. But! I have *great* hair."

My voice trailed off. Michael's friend looked at me, her eyes wide. Michael stared at me, his jaw dropped.

Eventually the two of them picked up conversation on a different topic that had nothing to do with bad television or crazy wives, but I didn't recover as quickly. I sat mutely, antisocially as I asked myself, *"Where in the world did THAT come from?"*

• • • • •

It's probably safe to say not many people respond to a compliment by reciting an episode of an '80s sitcom. However, I know many *have* accepted a compliment with a litany of reasons of why the compliment giver was mistaken. Regardless of the tactic, the question remains: In a moment when someone is offering their respect, awe, or even adoration, why do we shower upon them all of the insecurities that have been holding us back?

Why don't we simply say "Thank you" and stop?

That July afternoon, on the sidewalk outside a café in Coronado, I anxiously waited for the friend to excuse herself from the table so I could begin the process of erasing the whole conversation from my memory. But it still makes me cringe when I think of it. Perhaps it's for the better, because the next day I purchased a hat. And for the rest of the weekend whenever someone commented on my fabulous hat, I simply said "Thank you."

And stopped.

LIABILITIES

My mother was going in for a procedure of some kind.

It was minor.

I wasn't worried.

That is... until I told Michael.

Michael and I had been dating for just shy of a month. He was in California, I was in the bedroom of my apartment in Arizona folding clothes and putting them away, and we were on the phone. I told him about the procedure. He asked if it was serious. I told him it was minor. He asked if she would be put under. I said, yes I think so. He paused, and then proceeded to tell me a horror story of the time his mother had been put under. The story went on and on and on and on and finally ended with, "I didn't know if I would ever see her alive again."

Silence.

"Kindra?" Nothing. "Kindra?" Nothing. He paused. I could hear his thought process through the phone. "However..." he started slowly. "I'm sure that your mother will be fine. I'm sure everything with your mother will go as planned...."

Michael has never been the best with words.

Thankfully my mother *was* fine; everything went as planned.

Sadly, Michael did not learn his lesson.

• • • • •

We had been dating approximately six months, and from the beginning we were pretty open about our individual financial standings for two reasons. 1) He was in charge of accounting at the company I worked for, so his signature was on my paycheck. No secrets there. 2) He was the one I would call in a panic when my bank account was overdrawn. Again.

However, though conversations about money were not uncommon, it didn't make them any less painful. Painful for both of us.

Michael was able to graduate from college with no student loans, no credit card loans, no car loans, no loans at all except for the condo loft he bought in the heart of Old Town Scottsdale. I, on the other hand, had $6,000 on a credit card, a car I could barely afford and (then upgraded when I got a raise and could afford *that* one even less), an apartment that I loved but was way out of my league, and just shy of $40,000 in student loans to pay off.

That's right, $40,000 in student loans.

Am I a doctor? No.
A lawyer? No.
A senior for four years? No.

I blame my loans on love. I blame most things in my life on love.

It began when I was a senior in high school. I hopped in a van with eight other high school seniors to take a four-hour trip northwest to Concordia College in Moorhead, Minnesota. Right on the other side of the river from Fargo (though if the movie didn't exist yet, was the city actually real?).

I don't remember much from that trip except that I saw the legendary Concordia Christmas Choir Concert, I found my way to the boys' dorms (where, at the time, you were only allowed to go on the weekends and Wednesday nights), and met a handsome boy named Tim. I got locked in a stairwell in the indoor track-gymnasium when I failed to read the sign that said "Emergency Exit Only Alarm Will Sound." Unfortunately Handsome Tim happened to be walking by at the very moment I started screaming and was the one to rescue me. Then I got lost, at night, in the snow, looking for the library on a campus that spanned a mere two blocks.

At first glance, it wasn't a great trip. But there was something about that place—that place that had an ear of corn for a mascot. Something that took me in and never really let me go. It was love.

Love... and the $20,000+ a year tuition—a price tag that would seem to never let me go; to hang over my head for years to come.

I'm not exactly sure how it all went down. I remember choosing Concordia. I remember getting a nice scholarship, but not nice enough. I remember working all summer as a beer cart girl at my hometown golf course. I remember working my freshman year making outbound cold-calls to high school seniors to see if they wanted to spend $20,000+ a year on their education. I remember working nights and weekends at the Outback Steakhouse where I always reeked of beer and beef. I remember opening a savings account and depositing money in it but apparently it wasn't enough because at the end of those four years, before interest, I owed $21,000.

Yes. That's only half of my debt.

The other half happened in the fall of 2003, when I started graduate school at New Mexico State University. Why did I decide to go there? In addition to their great communication program, 1) Because they accepted me as a graduate assistant so my tuition was discounted and I was paid a stipend. 2) Because it was a bargain. Everything in New Mexico is a bargain. And 3) It was as far away from the Fargo winter as I could go.

Out of habit, I filled out the student loan paperwork. And what do you know? Without any signatures from my parents, without any trouble at all, I was approved for an $8,000 loan. I was pretty sure I had won the lottery. Since my education itself cost somewhere around $5,000, I would have plenty of money left over to buy tickets to visit my boyfriend in Minnesota every other weekend. And I did. All for love.

By the time the money cart came rolling around campus the next year, I had already broken up with the Minnesota boyfriend. So instead of for the love of a man, I took out the *second* $8,000 for the love of shoes and going out to eat.

That's right, $10,000 worth of education and $16,000 in student loans, bringing my student loan grand total to $37,000.00.

While conversations about money were common between Michael and me, they weren't any less painful. Painful for me because I was bleeding $500 a month into these debts and getting nowhere; painful for Michael because, for a man who still had his savings from his first paper route, it hurt to be in love with a woman who, though she made plenty of money, didn't have a penny to her name (and didn't really seem to care).

• • • • •

Perhaps this was weighing particularly heavy on his mind that night as we walked into our favorite sushi joint six months into our heavenly relationship. We sat

down at the sushi bar, ordered our drinks, turned in
our raw fish desires, and then he turned to me to speak.

"Kindra, you know... I come with a lot of assets. You
come with a lot of liability."
He said it very matter-of-factly. He said it with no warning. He said it right to my face. As if it were a perfectly
normal way to start a conversation with your girlfriend
of six months.

I stared at him. I squinted my eyes. I didn't move.

Who did this guy think he was?!
I was too insulted to hold back tears.
I was too angry to cry.
I just sat there, staring at him, wondering if next he
would tell me that my mother was going to die.

• • • • •

One slow, Saturday night I was at home and, out of
pure laziness for not wanting to search for the remote, I
was watching *The Suze Orman Show* – the show about
money and financial fools.

The woman is intense.

I don't necessarily agree with everything she says, (though I thoroughly enjoy her "Can I Afford It?" bits), but that slow Saturday night, love her or hate her, Suze said something that stuck with me.

(Picture the following statement in Suze Orman's voice. Please. It's much more fun that way).

Money goes where there is power. If you are living off someone else, if you are living off your credit cards, if you are living off money that isn't actually yours to begin with, you have no power. You are powerless. What's worse than being powerless? The fact that money will never come to you. You have to shift the pendulum of power with your own actions. Live lean. Live lean until you're living on your own money. Then, then! will the power return, then! will money start coming to you once again.

However hurtful it was to hear "you come with liability," it was true. More than just my debt, it was the way I was living; always out of my means, but always sure I deserved the luxury I was financing and always sure it would work out in the end, somehow. I was living powerlessly. Until I turned that around, I *was* a liability.

It was time for that to change. Enough was enough.

• • • • •

The credit card was paid first.
Every spare dollar I had went to paying off IKEA furniture I had already sold on Craigslist.
The card was paid in full in February of 2008 (and strangely, Michael proposed in March).

After saving for a year for our wedding then eating, celebrating, and dancing the completely paid-for night away, every spare dollar we had went to paying off the student loans.

On May 19, 2009, just shy of six weeks after our wedding, I owed three different institutions $23,998.78 for my long-since-completed education. We used Dave Ramsey's "Snowball Theory" and paid off the smaller amounts first. If you can believe it, it was actually fun. Fun to watch the amounts tick down. Fun to not buy things I otherwise would have.

In January of 2010, I owed $20,737.84.

By February I paid off one of the loans entirely and then put *that* money toward the *next* loan. I didn't go shop-

ping, Michael made us cook at home, and like a snow-
ball racing down a hill, the rate at which my balance
decreased gained momentum.

On March 11, 2010, I owed $14,570.28.
On April 26, 2010, I owed $12,010.26.

More and more started going to the principal balance
until it was only pennies being paid to interest.

On June 3, 2010, I owed $7,159.92—a mere third of
what it had been a year earlier. On June 5, with the
help of our delayed tax return, I wiped out the last of
the Concordia loans. I heard of another friend who went
to Florida with her tax return. *Before*, I would have
been jealous, *now* all I could think was how fleeting her
happiness was, and how *my* happiness seemed to be
snowballing as quickly as my loans were melting away.

That summer, all that remained were my biggest
mistakes. The rest of my $16,000 worth of plane tickets
I shouldn't have paid for and shoes I no longer had.
On June 25, 2010 I checked some of the stats on this
final loan. On one screen it read: *Your loan has been
prepaid and your automatic payment has been moved
to reflect this prepayment. Your next payment is due*

August 28, 2013.

August 28. 2013. The magnitude of the moment hit me. I had just purchased three years of my life back.

On June 29, 2010 I made my final payment of $912.38. On July 5th my account read: *Paid in Full.*

• • • • •

Sitting next to Michael at the sushi counter, being told I was a liability, is something I will never forget. An ugly moment became a beautiful catalyst for change. However, some things never change... because though this is indeed a story about financial independence, it is also a story about love.

That night, six months into our relationship and immediately after the liability comment, Michael continued— as genuine and unedited as he had started.

By identifying our current roles (he the asset, me the liability) he was stating a point of reference; so that, "Years down the road when you are bringing in the big money with all of your talents, and I'm still working a steady job with a steady income... years down the road when you are the biggest asset we have ever known, I want you to remember where we started."

He was more concerned about my assets all along.

And from that moment on, he referred to the student loans as "ours."

THE UNOFFICIAL TICKET MASTER

I remember the first time I saw the Golden Gate Bridge.

It left me breathless.

Love at first sight.

From that moment on, though I was not a fan of clouds, or rain, or mist, or fog, I loved San Francisco. I loved the pace of the city, the tall buildings that were made taller by the endless hills. I loved the sunglasses sold on the street that got cheaper the more pairs I purchased. I loved the seals that sat on the pier, barking their woes to the tourists who stood listening. I loved everything about the city.

Everything except *getting* there.

Because getting there meant taking the BART.

Which meant facing the BART ticket machine.

The truth is, I have never been very good at public
transportation. I drive in the light rail lane while wondering why there are so many metal ruts in the street.
I get stuck in between the metal poles in the turnstiles
at subway stations. Once on a microbus in Mexico City I
had to throw myself to the pavement because I couldn't
figure out how to get the bus to stop. I rolled onto the
sidewalk, clutching the fanny pack hidden beneath my
skirt, while the driver yelled, "God Bless Ame-ree-ca."

However, I do not necessarily believe these public trans-
port failures were entirely my fault. How was I supposed
to know that the signs with a train on it meant a train
would be driving *on* the street, that I was supposed
to move quickly and with force through the metal
gateways, or that the little cord overhead signaled the
driver? Was there a *class*? A study guide? No. And the
BART station was no different.

The BART Experience begins with a ticket machine. A
machine that dispenses tiny, yet absolutely necessary,
scraps of paper. A machine that, no matter what buttons
you push or how many dollars you insert, you are doing
something wrong. To make matters worse, the strug-

gling never happened in private. All the while you fight with the machine, there is the haunting feeling that someone was watching. And in fact, someone *is*.

He is a nameless man. A tall, lanky, seen-better-days African-American man in his mid-forties. He wears a baseball cap turned backward, baggy windbreaker pants and coat. He carries with him a large duffel bag, the bottom of which sinks in the middle as if he's carrying something small, but heavy. He walks up and down the vending machines "assisting" people with their tickets.

It was on a trip with Michael that I saw the man for the first time. As he paced back and forth, I thought how brilliant it was that the BART hired attendants to help weary travelers with the ticket machines, a move that certainly would enhance the overall customer experience. I thought the attendant uniform could use some work, but otherwise, for the most part, this seemed to be a good move.

It was in the middle of this thought process that Michael informed me that the tall, lanky man was not an *employee*. No. He was just *there*. There to take advantage of those who didn't know any better.

Well. That certainly wasn't going to be us.

We patiently stood in line, with masses of other travelers, awaiting our turn to wrestle the machine and secure our passage into the great city via the BART. Some people were seamless, others struggled, and towering above them all was the Unofficial BART Ticket Master. We tried not to make eye contact with him as he hovered. Instead, we peered over the shoulders of the people ahead of us, hoping to catch a glimpse of the correct combination of buttons to push.

Finally it was our turn. Michael stepped up to the machine, took a deep breath, and bravely pushed a button on the touchtone screen.
The machine answered with an angry beep.

He pushed another. Another angry beep. More buttons. The machine was getting louder as it beeped in protest. As Michael continued pushing buttons, more frantically this time, the Towering Ticket Master heard the beeps-of-despair and made his way to our machine.

"Hurry, hurry, he's coming," I hissed in panic. Michael was sweating, I was shaking, and the machine continued to beep—a cackling laughter of sorts.

"Come on. Come on." Michael pleaded with the machine. He was like a kid on an elevator now, pushing any button he could find.

"Need help?" the voice came from above.

"Nope, nope we're good, we're good," Michael responded, never a fan of a guy looking to make a buck for no good reason. He gave me that 'don't make eye contact' look again.

"Money first," the voice came again.

"What? Oh. Money." Michael fumbled for his wallet. He was cracking. The pressure was getting to him. I kept looking at the ground.

"Where you goin'?"

Unsure if it was safe to say, but more unsure that we would ever get there if I didn't, I whispered, "Embarcadero."

"OK." With that the Ticket Master took over. "Put in your money." We put in $10. "You want two tickets." Push button, push button, fast as lightening he did. "$3.80

one way to Embarcadero." Push button, push button. Pow. Bang. "Decrease amount by $2.40 cents in 5 cent increments." Beep boop beep boop beep boop, the machine was happily responding to these familiar fingers. "And there you go."

"Huh." said Michael. He was utterly speechless.

The machine started to buzz, two tickets came out, and the sound of change came clanging down the chute.

"That's your change right there..." the man started to say, as I started to reach for it. Michael's hand stopped me.

"Naw man, that's yours."

As we started to walk away, the Ticket Master thanked us then asked (I believe genuinely concerned), "Do you know how to get *on* the BART?"

Michael smiled. "Yeah, we got it. Thanks."

As we pulled our luggage behind us and stuck our ticket through the machine to open the gate to the BART, Michael said (almost to himself), "Wow. That man *actually* provided a service. He *actually* brought value to the market."

We stepped on the escalator and rode up to the platform where a weekend in the Golden Gate City awaited. However, despite multiple dinners at restaurants, entire afternoons of shopping, and endless customer service encounters, no one offered more assistance or provided more value than the Unofficial Ticket Master. And though it was only a handful of change, he *earned* every dime of it.

• • • • •

In business, the greatest successes are those companies, those individuals who truly provide value to their customers and to the marketplace as a whole. They do this through innovation, through strong customer service, and by simply identifying needs and fulfilling them. There is nothing more refreshing than finding someone who is truly adding value by making your life better, easier, more fulfilling. When evaluating professional worth, I now ask myself this: Am I providing value? If so, how much? And how can I provide more?

Or I just ask this: Am I as valuable to my customer as the guy at the BART was to me? If the answer is yes, I know I'm on the right track.

MEETING AMBER

The pressure was on.

I was meeting a friend of a professional contact and it was imperative that I make a good first impression. The pressure was on, but I wasn't worried.... I could be *super* charming when I needed to be—I had lots of funny jokes I could tell, and I always laughed loudly at others' jokes in return.

The woman I was to meet was named Amber, and before meeting her I was given a debriefing. Amber was quiet and soft-spoken. She didn't respond well to a lot of energy and preferred to communicate with people who speak in calm, soft, even tones. She was often off-put by boisterous laughter. Gestures were best kept to a minimum and should not extend beyond the immediate frame of the body. Smiling was okay, but not recommended.

Basically, Amber was the Anti-Kindra.
I wanted to back out, but it was too late.
Shortly after the Amber rundown, I found myself at the restaurant chosen for my "encounter." I opened the heavy door and took a few deep breaths, chanting quietly to myself, "I am as soothing as a summer day, as calming as a trickling stream, as soft as a bunny, as light as a feather, as stiff as a board."

As I walked into the main dining area I saw her, the woman I knew must be Amber. I tiptoed up to her in my silver ballerina slipper shoes (the quietest shoes I own), gently extended my hand and slowly slid into my chair. Unfortunately, my attempt at grace and serenity was thwarted by the chair, which squealed on the stained concrete floor. I grabbed the edge of the table in an effort to balance myself but instead thrust enough uneven weight to the back two legs of the chair that the front legs came up and nearly propelled me back-of-skull-first onto the concrete floor. The entire restaurant turned to stare as I toppled to the floor, silent silver ballerina slippers pointed straight to the ceiling.

Though my body was spared injury, my composure was not. Any hope I had had of impressing Amber with my calming personality was gone. I blushed. With little other choice, I decided it was probably better to just be plain old Kindra. So I was.

I sat there with Amber that afternoon and after deciding (or rather having no other choice but) to be myself, I noticed a very distinct difference between the Amber I *thought* I was meeting and the Amber who sat in front of me. Amber was vivacious and quick witted. She spoke loudly, passionately and freely. Her excitement for life oozed out of every exaggerated gesture. She laughed boisterously, frequently, and was a huge fan of the many jokes she herself cracked. She was nothing like I thought she'd be....

She wasn't the Anti-Kindra. In fact, it was almost as if she was a reflection.

As our conversation continued, a corner of my mind wandered to an old Japanese proverb I had once heard, a proverb that had suddenly come to life. This is the story as I remember it:

There once was a large hill and at the top of the hill was rumored to be a small house nestled deep in the woods. The house was not easy to find, but the rare traveler who dared to seek it and succeeded would be rewarded with a gift: the complete understanding of the kind of world he lived in. Many a story had been told about this place in the two towns that rested on either side of the great hill. The stories were shared sitting cozy around fireplaces to humans and pets a like.

One evening a grouchy, scowling, skulking pup in one of the towns decided he would go seek his reward at The House of a Thousand Mirrors. Slowly he made his way up the hill. He put one paw in front of the other and mumbled, "The weather sure is miserable today. Then again, the weather is always miserable. The birds sure are annoying today. Then again, they're always annoying." He grumbled and walked until the pup finally found his way to The House of a Thousand Mirrors.

Slowly, he climbed the old creaky stairs and pushed open the old creaky door. Finally he was there, standing inside The House of a Thousand Mirrors. It was dark. He couldn't see a thing. "I shoulda known," he moaned, "all this time, all this traveling, for nothing."

Just then, the room was filled with three bursts of light and sound (that were far too electronically advanced for this ancient little hut, but so the story goes). The room was illuminated; a thousand mirrors came to life, all at once.

But the scowling pup did not notice the mirrors.... All he saw were the faces of a thousand pups staring back at him as unhappy as he had ever been and a thousand times worse. He growled at them, they growled back. He bared his teeth, they bared back. He started to lunge at them, and a thousand pups lunged back with evil in their eyes.

The pup let out a yelp and raced out of the little house. As he reached the old creaky door, the lights went dark, the dogs disappeared, and the pup started the long walk home alone.

"That is a miserable place. I will never return. Filled with miserable mangy pups. I will never return."

A few evenings later a perky, playful, little dog who lived in the village on the other side of the hill decided he would go seek his reward at The House of a Thousand

Mirrors. He bounded up the hill wagging his tail furiously and panting with glee. He danced one paw in front of the other saying, "What a beautiful day for an adventure."

Finally, he reached the house he had been seeking. He quickly climbed the old creaky stairs. With nervous excitement he pushed open the old creaky door with his little wet nose. Finally he was there, standing inside The House of a Thousand Mirrors.

It was dark. He couldn't see a thing. "Oh boy, oh boy," he whispered, "I just can't wait. Oh boy, oh boy, this is just too exciting."

Just then, the room was filled with three bursts of light and sound. The room was illuminated; a thousand mirrors came to life, all at once.

But the perky, playful, friendly pup did not notice the mirrors.... All he saw were the faces of a thousand pups staring back at him as friendly as he had ever been and a thousand times more so. He barked at them, they barked back. He wagged his tail, they wagged back. He started to hop about in circles, yipping yapping as playful dogs do, and a thousand pups hopped about in circles, excited to have a new playmate.

This went on for some time—the yipping, the yapping the hopping about. Eventually, the excitement was all too much and he was starting to get hungry. He bid farewell to his thousand friends and as he reached the old creaky door, the lights went dark, the dogs disappeared, and the friendly pup started the long walk home alone.

"That is a *wonderful* place. I will return soon. Filled with so many wonderful pups. I will return soon."

I left the meeting with Amber that afternoon, pleased. Though I had intended to make a good impression on *her*, meeting Amber left a lasting impression on *me*. It occurred to me that my professional friend who asked that I meet Amber in the first place was a fairly quiet, soft-spoken woman who didn't respond well to a lot of energy. The Amber she knew was merely a reflection of *herself*. Just as the Amber I knew was a reflection of *me*.

For better or worse, so much of the world we live in is simply a reflection. We must be careful the face, be aware the attitude, be mindful the disposition we take with us as we go about our days because, as if we were standing in a house of a thousand mirrors, it will be reflected back a thousand times or more.

RAW FISH AND A LITTLE BLACK DRESS

I love sushi.

When at a sushi spot, trendy or not, I order way more than is fashionable and shove as much raw fish in my mouth as will fit. I could eat sushi every day, and believe me, I've tried. I went a full week once—sushi every day for seven days. *Amazing* and—though I suffered from the inevitable salt swell for days after—totally worth it.

Unfortunately, Michael isn't a *huge* fan of going out to eat so my sushi obsession is never fully satisfied. If only I could make sushi in the comfort of my own home. But that seemed complicated.

• • • • •

On the day before my birthday, I went shopping. I invited Michael to join me just in case he needed any last-minute gift ideas for the big day. He met me at my favorite outdoor mall on a beautiful February afternoon, and we wandered through a few of the shops and boutiques. It was an educational tour. I pointed out things I liked and informed him of colors that looked best on me: coral, lemon yellow, and a specific shade of royal blue. We eventually found ourselves in Macy's where he put his new knowledge to the test. While he chose teal instead of royal, and mustard instead of lemon, he did correctly identify coral. He found a casual baseball T-shirt with three-quarter-length coral colored sleeves. I offered positive reinforcement for his good work, then moved away from the T-shirt before he got the wrong idea... a baseball Tee, regardless of color wasn't exactly what I had in mind for a birthday gift.

On our way out of the shopping center, we made one final stop at high-end boutique. This was a bad decision and I knew it. There was absolutely nothing in that store I could justify buying on a whim, and I knew there was nothing in there that my money-conscious husband would consider buying *ever*. However, I mindlessly made my way to the back of the store. And that's when it happened....

I fell in love.

I fell in love with a little black cocktail dress created just. for. me.

I'm not sure if it was the funhouse—make your legs look waaaay longer than they actually are—mirrors, or if it was the three sales girls telling me that, of all the girls who had ever tried on the dress, it had never looked so good. It could have been that I was just recovering from the stomach flu and could fit into a size two, or even the little gasp I thought I heard Michael let out when I stepped out to show him.... Whatever it was, I *had to have* that dress. And I had faith that it would be mine.

You see, in the Birthday Department, Michael owed me. The year before, he had forgotten my birthday. Over half the day had passed before he said "the words" or sang "the song," and when he finally remembered, he gave me a pair of generic flip-flops instead of the special butt-shaping sandals I had asked for, and a bra—a bra *I* had already purchased with *my* money but that *he* put in a box, wrapped, and called it a gift.

After many tears on my end and endless apologies on his, I gave Michael a speech he will never forget.

"*A birthday is a day to feel special. A day to celebrate the
fact that you are here, that you are you. A day when the
ones you love let you know just how much they love you.
On my next birthday, I don't care WHAT you get me, as
long as I feel special.*"

That little black dress, all three hundred and sixty-eight
dollars of it, would make me feel *very* special.

As we left the boutique that afternoon and went our
separate ways to our cars, Michael said he would 'meet
me at home.' And though he was trying to hide it, I knew
he was going back into the mall. I knew he was going
back to buy that dress. I didn't even care that it was the
day before my birthday and he was only *now* buying my
gift... that dress would be mine.

• • • • •

My birthday started out spectacularly. Michael's first
breath was spent shouting HAPPY BIRTHDAY at the
top of his lungs before the sun had even peeked above
the horizon. I smiled, I felt special. Then he took me to
Starbucks. I found us a table as he ordered our drinks
and when he came back he also had one of the mini
donuts with sprinkles on top I had been drooling over
for months but never allowed myself to eat. He smiled.

"Happy Birthday."

In that small moment, I felt so special.
I couldn't wait until it was time to start opening gifts.

Michael soon left for work and I spent the rest of the
morning in spin and yoga classes. There, they played my
favorite songs and I hung out with some of my favorite
people. When I finished, I walked to my car to find a
single rose on the windshield.

I felt so special.

As I pulled into our driveway, I saw another rose awaiting me; laying in the middle of the driveway. Under
different circumstances it could have been considered a
little creepy but on that day, I felt *so* special.

I walked into our home, excited for more surprises,
wondering if the roses were leading me to a big dress-
shaped box. Seeing no box and hungry from working
out, I opened the fridge. There was a rose. I grabbed a
yogurt and went to my computer. There was a rose. I
grabbed my computer bag to get the power cord. There
was a rose. Michael had placed a rose on every stop of
my morning ritual path until I had a collection of twelve.

Even when I went to the bathroom to shower; I lifted the lid of the toilet.... There was a rose in the bowl. Even then, fishing a flower out of the toilet, I felt special.

By the end of the day I was beside myself. I knew that this was going to be the best birthday ever. Donuts, roses, and the best was yet to come. I just knew it.

That evening, Michael came home from work, his arms filled with grocery bags, a bottle of Pinot Noir, and a box with two of my favorite cupcakes in it. He announced as he set the goods down in the kitchen, "Tonight, in honor of the birth of my beautiful wife, we stay *in* for dinner. Tonight, we make sushi."

Wow.

The next hour was spent drinking wine, cooking rice, shredding carrots and cucumber, cutting avocados, slicing tuna and salmon, spreading rice on seaweed wraps and creating sushi masterpieces. We laughed and played and ate the pieces of raw fish that weren't suitable for rolling. Once the sushi was made and the soy sauce was properly mixed with ginger and wasabi, we carried our dinner into the living room, onto the coffee table, where we would feast.

However, even after all of that, there was still something on my mind and the anticipation was killing me. Before we started eating, I asked in my sweetest voice, "Michael, is it time for me to open my presents?" The pitch of my voice got gradually higher as I spoke and by the word 'presents' it was so high only dogs and husbands could hear it.

"Aha! Yes! Just one second!" With that, Michael ran back into the kitchen, removed the cupcakes from their box and set them each on the counter. He then disappeared with the empty box into the bedroom. He emerged no fewer than thirty seconds later, still holding the cupcake container. He set the box on the coffee table in the living room next to the sushi. "Happy Birthday," he said with a smile, and I could tell he was proud.

I, however, was slightly confused. Even though the dress I tried on *was* a Size Flu, I still wasn't sure how it would fit in that tiny little box. Maybe he made a "Dress Treasure Hunt" and this was the first clue that would tell me to go look in the closet. I opened the box.

And there it was.
The gift Michael had gone back into the mall to get.
The gift I had been waiting for all day long....

A casual baseball T-shirt with three-quarter length coral colored sleeves.
Price tag included.

Hmmm.

"Remember?! You said you liked this one," his face was eager and pleased.

"Yes, yes. I remember." I was trying to remain calm.... "Are there any more presents?" With that second high-pitched question I was holding out hope that he had purchased *both* the shirt *and* the dress in honor of (as he had put it) the birth of his beautiful wife.

"Now that you mention it" (the angels began singing), "there is something else." Michael went back in the kitchen and emerged, for the final time, with the rest of the gifts for my twenty-ninth birthday.

Fancy chopsticks with which to eat my homemade sushi.
A Japanese fan to keep myself cool as I ate my homemade sushi.
A Japanese parasol to hold while I enjoyed my homemade sushi.

He was thrilled.

I was devastated.

I tried to hide my disappointment, but the rush of tears streaming down my face apparently gave it away. When he asked what was wrong, I blubbered something about him not caring about my birthday more than to shove a shirt with a tag in a cupcake box and he hadn't learned anything from the year before.

(Even as I write that statement, I am embarrassed and ashamed.)

In the moments that followed, a confused Michael tried to calm his irrational bride. "Kindra," he said, his voice soft. "You said a birthday is about feeling special. I tried to do that. All day. I'm sorry if I failed."

It was then that I remembered my birthday speech from the year before; a speech he had remembered. A speech I had apparently forgotten.

"A birthday is a day to feel special. A day to celebrate the fact that you are here, that you are you. A day when the ones you love let you know just how much they love you. On my next birthday, I don't care WHAT you get me, as

long as I feel special."

• • • • •

It has been said in many ways; the good life is not measured in things, but measured in precious moments. Sitting there—a sushi feast before me, a wonderful man beside me—I realized that I had failed myself. Memories from the day scrolled across my mind: The early morning birthday wish, the donut, the rose after rose after rose, the sushi, the wine, the favorite cupcakes, the coral shirt, even the parasol, fan, and chopsticks for a full sushi experience…. He had done exactly as I had asked, exactly as I had always wanted. Dress or no dress, I felt special the whole day through. He had spent the entire day showing me how much he loved me. That is really the best any of us can hope for as we leave one year behind and begin another.

"I'm sorry. I'm so sorry," didn't seem like enough, but it was all I knew to say. With a wasabi-laced kiss, we put the dress fiasco behind us. We spent the rest of the evening gorging ourselves on the fruits (the fish) of our labor, drinking wine, and whapping each other with my Asian umbrella.

Sushi had never tasted so good.

That was Monday. On Wednesday, I went back and bought the dress for myself. Happy Birthday to me.

THE STORY OF THE FANCY CHECKS

When I was fourteen years old, a box arrived on our front doorstep. It was addressed to my mother. Actually, it was four small boxes wrapped in plain brown paper. Never judge a box by its wrapping. Inside the boxes was a great treasure.

Checks.

Not just any checks though. Not the plain, grayish-colored, bank-issued checks I was used to. No, these were the most amazing checks I had ever seen. They had four different images on them. A lush, green forest. A summer's day sky. The desert. The ocean. I was obsessed with these checks. While it is certainly not unusual for children to have some level of fascination with their parents' bank accounts, my fascination had nothing to do with money. I *loved* those checks. I would sit and flip through them, one by one. Forest. Sky. Desert. Ocean. Forest. Sky. Desert. Ocean. Forest.Sky.Desert.Ocean. I dreamt of the day when I could get colorful checks.

One immediate issue: I had no bank account. At fourteen, I had no job, therefore, no money, therefore, no need for a bank account, therefore, no need for fancy checks.

But there was hope.

Two years later I turned sixteen.
When I was sixteen, I got my first job.
With my first job, I earned my first money.
With my first money I was allowed to open my first checking account.
And with my first checking account...

I remember the first question I asked my mother, as we walked out of the bank and back to the car:

"When can I choose my special checks?"

"Kindra, I didn't get special checks until I was forty," my mother responded.

Ugh.

I know it sounds stupid. I know it sounds very "sixteen," but I was really bummed. I wanted those special checks. I didn't want to wait until I was forty. I thought I did everything I was supposed to do. Didn't that mean I should get the thing I wanted?

I was bummed and, a little embarrassed that I had been so foolish. Foolish to believe, to *expect*, that I could have fancy checks at my young age. Obviously special checks were something you had to earn. Something you had to wait years, a *lifetime*, to have.

It was a quiet ride home from the bank.

• • • • •

I was in email conversation with a friend of mine, seeking his counsel.

As an experienced and respected entrepreneur, this friend had the career I wanted and a life I envied: books, speaking, travel, and the privilege of improving people's lives with his message. He had a loving wife, a beautiful family and the flexibility to enjoy all of it. I watched his life like I had once paged through my mother's books of beautiful checks—with dreamy adoration. Every time we talked, I asked my friend lots of questions and with every answer I made my list of Things to Do to Have the Best Life Ever.

I knew it would be mine. Any day now, it would be mine.

And then, somewhere in the email back-and-forth, my enviable friend said this:

"I worked for 20 years and now I am *finally* pursuing my passion... it'll be exciting when you are *finally* able to pursue yours."

Finally?

As ridiculous as it sounds, I was suddenly 16 again. I was sitting in my mother's car in the bank parking lot thinking I was within moments of achieving a long-sought goal only to learn I was still 20 years away. How could I have been so foolish? Foolish to believe, to *expect*, that I could pursue my passion *now*. If my brilliant friend had to wait 20 years, certainly I did too.

In the days following, that email weighed heavy on my mind. I tried to remember other times I had felt that way—defeated, disappointed, so far away from what I wanted—and how I handled it. That is when I remembered the Fancy Check incident, and what happened after I left the bank...

• • • • •

After that long, silent car ride home, I devised a plan. I knew I was a long way from forty and therefore a long way from special checks, however, I wanted to be prepared for when that day came. Every Sunday morning I would shake the pages of the paper until the 'check ad' with hundreds of check options on it came loose. This drove my father crazy because it got the paper all messy, but I didn't care. I would stare at this advertisement, analyzing the designs—Garfield, Mickey, hearts, flowers, nature, weird cartoon baby images—and debate which one I wanted, which one I would get when I turned forty.

Eventually I started saving the ads, pulling them out of the drawer in my night table before I went to sleep. Then, I started *comparing* the check companies—who offered more checks for a better price? What were the check trends from week to week, month to month? Which checks came with the most free stuff: return labels, checkbook cases, stickers with the letter K in fancy script?

Finally, I started doing the math. How much money would I have to save before I was able to buy the fancy checks? Should I start saving now? And that's when I realized...

Fancy checks weren't that expensive.

Really. I could work one afternoon at the drive-in restaurant and earn enough for ten boxes of them. Which begged the question, If the *expense* of the checks wasn't the reason for the Not Till You're Forty barrier, what was?

The truth: Forty was some invisible line my mother had drawn based on her own experience and passed on to me. Nothing more. It was *my* decision whether or not I wanted to adopt that barrier, that belief, for myself.

I decided I didn't want to.

By the end of the summer, at the age of sixteen and after careful deliberation, I had ordered my first round of fancy checks. They had four different patterns of lines drawn with brightly colored crayons. Simple. Classy. The most beautiful checks I'd ever seen. And though it's been years since the last time I cared what was on my checks, the feeling I had that day—sixteen and victorious—is one I haven't forgotten. When discouraged in the face of irrelevant barriers and other people's (albeit well-meaning) timelines, I think back to the wisdom of a younger me. I carefully weigh my options and take measured steps towards what I desire and, with great anticipation, look forward to that feeling of satisfaction I had the day four plain brown-wrapped boxes arrived on the doorstep.

Four boxes of fancy checks, addressed to me.

WITH
AN I

I had a run-in at the open bar at a wedding with a girl in a Pepto-Pink dress.

The reception was about one hour from over and the bar had just run out of vodka, tequila, white wine, champagne and everything else delicious. A group of women had gathered, wondering if we'd be forced to drink beer. Just before we lost all hope, I noticed a few tall bottles standing in the back. While some of them were your standard (disgusting) whiskeys, one bottle read: ZEN.

ZEN? My (limited) yoga experience told me this could be a good thing.

As it turned out ZEN is a green tea liqueur. Upon my request, the bartender mixed it with the fresh-squeezed lemonade that had been rendered useless since the vodka ran out. I grabbed a short straw, mixed it until it was Ecto-Cooler green, and took a sip.

It was AMAZING. I held it high above my head in victory.

"This drink is AMAZING!" I shouted. "It is called... The Kindra!" (Creative beverage naming was never my strength.)

The rest of the women in line started cheering and, clamoring for a glass of The Kindra. Within moments they pulled out a second bottle of ZEN as more women wanted the bright green elixir. It was then that I turned to the woman in the Pepto-Pink bridesmaidish dress.

"Have you tried this drink?" I was excited.

"Ew. What is it?" she sneered.

"It's ZEN green tea liqueur and lemonade! It's called The Kindra!" I was excited.

"You should call it The Zendra."

It was a good name.

"Oh! That's a good name! The ZENDRA!" I was excited.

"Yes. And it's easier to say," she said with a snide smile.

Easier to say than... Kindra?

But. Kindra, Kindra is my *name*...

I may have been a little tipsy, but I could still identify an insult even if it was dressed in pink. I lowered my eyes, took another sip, and walked away.

• • • • •

It has not been an easy ride for my name and me.

When I was five I wanted to be named Nicole.

It was summertime. My mother, father and my little brother—who wore his blonde hair like a helmet on his head—drove the f o u r t e e n h u n d r e d miles from Scandia, Minnesota, to Pawleys Island, South Carolina. Our chariot: a 1980ish, two-door, yellow outside, black (vinyl) inside, Ford Escort.

I don't remember how long we were in South Carolina or which distant family relative we were visiting. I vaguely remember seeing the ocean for the first time and wearing a rainbow swimsuit. I definitely remember there was a candy store next door. And I *do* remember a girl hanging out at the distant relative's home.

A girl named Nicole.

The details about Nicole's life—who she was, why she was there, if we were related—were irrelevant. All I cared about was that Nicole had a My Little Pony Dream Castle.

An actual castle where all of her My Little Pony ponies could play.
I had ponies.
I had lots of ponies.
But my ponies were forced to play among the sheets and blankets on my bed, not in a castle. Nicole's ponies could admire themselves in a full length mirror and drink from tiny pony goblets.

I wanted a Dream Castle more than anything.
Sadly, I concluded it must be a luxury available only to Nicoles.

One evening as my mother tucked me into the sheets that smelled of ocean waves, I expressed to her my deepest desire:

To be named Nicole.

She looked at me with her sea-gray eyes, tucked my humidity-curled hair behind my ears and said, "Oh sweet pea, Kindra is a beautiful name. There are lots of Nicoles, but I have only known one Kindra and when you are a grown up, you will love having a name that no one has known before."

"But Mom, Kindra is kind of hard to say..."

She said nothing more, just kissed my forehead goodnight.

• • • • •

Nicole never caught on.
However, I did go by "Kindy" for much of my youth.
And no, if I did *not* know you in high school or college you can *never* call me that. Yes. I am serious.
On the first day of every grade, when teachers stumbled over Kindra, I told them, and all of my friends, to "just call me Kindy... like Cindy with a K."

I was Kindy until 2001.

In 2001, I interviewed for a serving position at the Out-
back Steakhouse in Fargo. I was waiting in one of those
wooden booths when the most beautiful man I had ever
seen walked out from the kitchen to join me. No, correc-
tion: to interview me. I was so taken by his dark eyes
and crooked smile, that when he read my name "Kindra"
off my application I simply nodded. I couldn't bring
myself to correct him. My name had never sounded so
beautiful.

I have been Kindra ever since.

At least I have tried to be.
There are times when, against my will, I am *Kendra*.

It seems no matter how clearly I try to enunciate, no
matter how strongly I stress that pivotal vowel, I often
end up as Kendra. And while it is a beautiful name, and
certainly more common, it's not *my* name. Nevertheless,
since it is only one letter, I usually let it go.
Usually.

• • • • •

I was in San Francisco and I agreed (against my better

judgment) to attend a bikram yoga class with my sister-in-law. On a Saturday morning we walked several blocks to an unassuming door and up a couple flights of stairs to the top floor of a warehouse/turned yoga studio. I approached the front desk and I let them know I was a first-timer. After acknowledging they "weren't responsible if I died" with a signature, the check-in girl called the instructor over to introduce her to her new victim. Me. Kindra.

"Welcome... Kendra? Kindra?" I nodded as she corrected herself.

The instructor spoke in a soothing voice as she told me a few of the "sensations" I might feel during my practice, including dizziness, nausea, shortness of breath, and seeing the proverbial light. Moments later I walked into a room of stench, situated my mat, put down my towel, and patiently stared at myself in the endless row of mirrors waiting, with fifty others, for class to begin. The instructor walked in, offered a few basic instructions and welcomed her new student.

"Everyone, we have a first-timer. Please welcome Kendra." She gestured in my direction and then turned to look me in the eye.

"Kendra, right?"

She was looking right at me, presumably deep into my being (the way only a yoga instructor can do). She was asking to be corrected if she was wrong—deep in her soul, she knew I wasn't a Kendra.

I looked back at her.

I heard a voice inside say, *Just say it. Just say Kindra. Just say "with an i."*

I heard another voice say, *Are you really going to interrupt class for one. letter?*

She was waiting for an answer. I nodded. I nodded again. That's fine. Kendra is fine. I can be Kendra.

• • • • •

We betray ourselves in small ways. With little neglects, small things we let slide. With lines we let people cross, or boundaries we never set. We betray ourselves when we choose not to speak up about whom we really are, what we really want, how we want to be understood by others. Even something as small as a name, a letter.

I betrayed myself that day. As soon as I let the moment pass, I knew I had made a mistake. I am not a Kendra. I am Kindra. I should never settle for less.

• • • • •

After the ninety-minute bikram class, we decided to walk down one of the many San Franciscan hills and treat ourselves to Starbucks; I thought it wise to follow dehydration with caffeine. I stood in line, and when it was my turn I asked the man behind the counter for a tall, nonfat, dark cherry mocha, with just one pump of dark cherry syrup and just one pump of mocha, and no whip cream (I know the order is a mouthful, but it just isn't right any other way).

He took a small cup off the stack and began furiously writing the details of my beverage. He finished, looked at me and said, "May I have your name please."

"Kindra."

I watched him as he began writing with the Sharpie on my cup. At no point did he pick up his pen to dot an "i"... this could only mean one thing. Kendra.

I could feel the two opposing forces within me start churning.
Just say "with an i."
Are you really going to hold up the line at Starbucks for a letter on a cup?

"ACTUALLY," I spurted with perhaps too much force. "Actually, it's Kindra. Kindra. With an i."

He stopped, Sharpie still in his hand. He stared at me over the thick glasses he wore on his wiry face. I looked at the long line of under-caffeinated people behind me and I immediately wished I had said nothing. *I take it back. Please. I'm sorry. Kendra is fine. I am not defined by a coffee cup.*

Just as I was about to say never mind, he spoke.

"Kindra.
"Kindra...

He paused. I held my breath.

"What a beautiful name." I exhaled a heavy breath as he threw away my first cup and wrote KINDRA on the second.

"I've never met a Kindra before. Beautiful. And as unusual as this drink you're ordering."

I walked out of Starbucks, proud. Though it was just a letter, it was a personal victory. I took a sip of my mocha and decided to name it "The Kindra."

ON THE BOTTOM OF THE PILE

I never considered myself a football fan.

Sure I went to all the high school games, but not for the football. I went to watch the boys.

I went to games in college too. But that was also about the boys.

And while I never considered myself a football fan, I *was* a big fan of the *season*. In Minnesota it meant the earth took on a different smell—a smell that meant homecoming dances and bonfires were near. A smell that meant, "Enjoy it now because soon you'll be freezing." Whether I watched the game or not, in my home football season felt warm and wholesome.

In my Minnesota home, during the Minnesota fall, my Minnesotan father watched the Minnesota Vikings. They were on the television in the living room in their proud purple and gold, and on the radio in the garage just in case he had to go outside to check on da John Deere tractor. For hours on Sundays we heard shouts for Warren Moon, or Dante Culpepper, or Randy Moss. My mom complained about "that noise" like it was her sacred Sabbath right to do so, while my dad made chicken wings or his traditional four-layer dip (we didn't need seven layers to get the job done), drank a Killian's Red and said "aw jeepers" in a disgusted, manly tone when the Vikes didn't come through.

Perhaps it's because I miss the change of season, or maybe it's because, in my adulthood, I've developed the need to yell at people and big men dressed in tights on television satisfies that need. Or it could be that I used "look at how cool I am sitting here watching football with you, don't you want to marry me?" as a means to impress Michael when we were dating and never broke the habit. Whatever the reason, over the years my football fan-ness evolved; so much so that eventually every Sunday afternoon I found myself sitting on my couch or at a sports bar eager to watch the game, any game, and cheer for or against *somebody.*

Cheering for the San Diego Chargers because that was Michael's team growing up. Cheering for the Arizona Cardinals to support the hometown team. Cheering *against* the Cowboys because of what Romo did to Jessica. Cheering *against* all things Manning. Cheering *against* the Saints because they play too dirty to call themselves saints. Cheering *against* the Packers because, duh, *always* cheer against *anything* Wisconsin (except cheese). And cheering *against* the Patriots for many reasons, not limited to their cheating and Tom Brady's desperate need for a haircut.

And like a good Minnesotan, I always cheer for the Vikings.

One Sunday afternoon early in the 2010-2011 season, I settled into the couch ready to cheer on the Purple and Gold. And though it was merely 10 a.m., I held nothing back, acting like a belligerent drunk in a bar even though I was sober on my own couch. I hollered at the mistakes, I posted witty Tweets, I cheered for the touchdowns, and paced the floor when it was time for a big play. Amidst all the excitement, the cheerleaders, the announcers who kept talking about how *old* Brett Favre was, the fumbles, the turnovers, the touchdowns, the injuries, there was one thing that stood out.

An unexpected lesson from an unlikely source.

On the Vikings team that year was a player named Adrian Peterson, who was pretty remarkable. To be honest, I wasn't a huge Peterson fan—I never understood what all the fuss was about. As far as I could tell, AP's entire job was to grab the football Brett Favre *handed* him—he didn't even have to *catch* it—and then run as fast as he could toward the goal line. The only problem was, most of the time, Adrian grabbed the ball and ran straight into a pile of men. A pile of huge, sweaty, opposite-team men who weren't about to let him go anywhere.

How irritating. How *boring.* I much preferred when the quarterback threw the ball forty yards to some lone catcher who then heroically tiptoed into the end zone. That's my kind of football. Unfortunately, it seemed every play Peterson got the ball, I was on my feet, screaming at the TV, my arms flailing in the air *"What?! Didn't you see that HUGE pile of HUGE men there?! What were you thinking?"* And every time they ignored my frustration as they pulled Adrian from the bottom of the pile over and over and over again.

That particular Sunday afternoon was no different. After a few beautiful passes, and then a few passes gone bad, it was back to the "Peterson on the Bottom of the Pile" strategy. However, during the replay of one of Peterson's one-yard-gain runs, stopped by a mob of very large men, the announcer said something that, in my *mind* I know was about football but in my *heart* I felt was about *me.*

"Peterson describes his job as famine, famine, famine, feast. There are going to be plenty of plays where he doesn't make progress, but all of them are leading up to plays that are game winners. He's okay with being patient. He knows it'll pay off."

Famine, famine, famine, feast.

I had barely had enough time to process the comment when, on the very next play Favre handed the ball to Peterson who took off like a rocket. He cut this way and that, jumped OVER defenders, and got all of us Vikings fans on our feet screaming the way we did when the Twins won the World Series in 1991. It was an EPIC play... an epic play that looked only *slightly* different from all the other times he was handed the ball and landed at the bottom of the pile. Only slightly. But that's all it takes to make a feast.

I know there are a lot of differences between myself and Adrian Peterson. He is slightly stronger, a little faster, significantly younger, and a little bit wealthier. But that Sunday, sitting on my Arizona couch watching Minnesota play, I felt that Adrian and I were one and the same.

Just like Peterson, my life often goes famine, famine, famine, feast. Though I much prefer the forty-yard pass and the graceful dance into the end zone, it doesn't always happen that way. Most of the time I am handed the ball and I run, trying to make a play, only to end up stuck on the bottom of a pile. Blocked. Come to think of it, most successes I have had have been preceded by many famine plays. That is simply how the game goes. If we can be patient and take on the famines, our feast is there and worth waiting for.

TWO TO TANGO

I only drank coffee on Saturday.

Every Saturday after spin class, two girlfriends and I
would sit at Mama Java's Coffeehouse until our hair
wreaked of roasting bean, we were shaking from refills,
and Michael had texted wondering if I died on the bike.
It was very Sex and the City—minus the city, minus
the liquor, minus one woman, plus sweaty sports attire
and smeared mascara. We informally took turns sharing stories of the week—work, men, friends, men, men.
Though two of us were married, there were still plenty of
men stories to share.

However, in the midst of endless men stories, one story

my single friend told stood out; perhaps because I'd
heard versions of it before, perhaps because it was a
story I had lived myself.

It starts with a man. A dreamy man. A charming man.
It continues with a beautiful woman. An intelligent
woman. She of course adores this man and he recipro-
cates that adoration... sometimes. When he feels like
it. And when he's not reciprocating, he always has a
reason.
He's stressed. Very stressed.
His friend is sad. He must help his sad, sad friend.
He's busy. Very busy. *So* busy that he *literally* does not
have *fifteen spare seconds* over the course of three days
to send a text.
Not one.
These are the reasons he cannot call, he cannot con-
nect, he cannot show this beautiful, intelligent woman
proper respect. These reasons are all good enough...
good enough when you don't know you deserve better.

It is never easy to sit at a table with your friends, male/
female, long-term/new-term friends as they tell you a
story and you already know the ending. On that particular Saturday, in that particular situation, I decided
to offer this:

It was freshman orientation, the summer before my first year of college. I traveled the four hours to see the campus I would soon call home. I met some of the students, spoke with some of the professors, made a few friends who I still know and love today. I also met "my future husband." Oh yes. He was fair-skinned, blonde-haired, blue-eyed, just what you would expect to find at a northern Minnesota Lutheran College. Interestingly enough, he had actually gone to my high school too; he was a senior when I was a freshman. And now, four years later, he was a senior (again) and I was a freshman (again). To my delight, he was more than willing to show me around campus while I was visiting. Then, later that summer, he came back to our hometown; he came over to my parents' house to see if I had any questions. The only question I could think of was, "Will I even see you when we get up to school?" His only answer, "Kindra, I hope we are *dating* when we get up to school."

As far as I was concerned, college was already a success—while I told my parents I wanted a diploma, secretly part of me just wanted a husband. I couldn't believe I had found him so quickly. I was pretty sure I didn't even need to go to school after all.

Unfortunately, within the first few weeks things started

going downhill. Apparently summer promises don't hold up well once the semester starts. I remember one Friday night we had made plans to go to dinner, but then an hour before I was to meet him outside the dorm, he called to say his grandmother had died. Awful. He wasn't going to be able to make it.

We rescheduled for the next Friday. Then, an hour before I was to meet him outside the dorm, he called to say his *other* grandmother died. Awful. He wasn't going to be able to make it.

I'll admit, I was taken aback by the coincidence. What are the chances he would lose both grandmothers within a week of each other? But I was sad for him all the same.

We rescheduled for the next Friday. And then a *third* grandma died.
Yes. A *third* one.

I was *pretty* sure something was up.

I thought I should get some outside advice. As I told this story to my roommate, to the girls in the bathroom, to the girls in my health class, to the girls on the speech team, their reactions were all the same. What a jerk! I should show up on his doorstep with a grief gift. What a jerk! I should offer to attend the funerals—all *three* of them. I should call his family and offer my condolences. What a jerk! It was unanimous. I agreed. What kind of a future husband behaves this way?

I planned to have words with him on the fourth Friday night of my college career. I was going to tell him that he should stop treating me like that. However, it would have to wait until after my Latin-Dance Competition for Spanish 3 class that evening.

· · · · ·

As my dance partner and I were warming up for the merengue, I told him about the triple dead grandmas. I told him what a jerk my future husband was. It was obvious the response I was hoping for, and I fully expected him to shout out "What a Jerk!" in Spanish. But he did not. He wasted no breath telling me I was right—he didn't even *touch* on the fact that my future husband was being a jerk. Instead, he responded: "Kindra, it takes two to tango."

Huh?

I should have known better than to talk to a man.

I didn't have time to clarify before we were strutting across the floor, though I don't think clarification would have helped. It wasn't until years later that I truly understood his meaning and it wasn't until years after *that* that I believed what he was saying was correct.

The tango is a passionate dance filled with twists and turns, but unless it is required for your grade in Spanish class, this dance is your *choice*. In these situations, in order for someone to be a jerk, you must be participating. You have to be waiting for the call that won't come, the text that won't be sent. In my story he might have been a jerk, but it was my decision to keep dancing; to keep calling, to keep engaging, to keep allowing myself to be treated that way. He was being a jerk, yes, but my heels were on, the rose tightly between my teeth. It is easy to blame your partner, but satisfaction/relief will never come unless you realize the role you play in your own struggle.

• • • • •

If you happen to be tangled in the tango as you read this, though we are not sitting at coffee, I hope the story of the dead grandmothers makes you laugh the way my friends did after spin that morning. My foolishness was funny. My second hope is that you'll take a look at your story, and just like my single friend did, take your final bow, exit stage right, and choose to end the dance.

THE OVERZEALOUS POST-IT

My dad loves famous people.

He loves meeting famous people or people who *know* famous people. He once met Kristi Yamaguchi's husband—it was big news. One day I waited on Kirby Puckett, the legendary Minnesota Twins baseball player, at the drive-in restaurant where I worked in high school and my dad talked about it for months.

If you ever call my father and say, "You'll never guess who I just met..." he will hang on every word, waiting for the famous-ness. You can hear his smile on the other end of the phone, his eyes twinkling. Most of the time this trait is annoying; embarrassing even, as he bumbles around like a giddy schoolgirl in the presence of even Y-List celebrities. However, there was one day, one fateful day, when my father's fame-foolishness was the only thing that could save me.

• • • • •

It was a Saturday morning as I stood in the lobby of the spin studio. I strapped on my shoes, talked to my friends, and watched the people come in the door. It was a typical Saturday morning until, as fate would have it, two people walked in who I had seen before but only from a distance. The color drained from my face, my heart started to pound, my mouth went dry as I wondered if it could really be them...

• • • • •

It was just one week earlier; Michael and I were at a charity event with several of our friends from spin. Toward the end of the program, an attractive couple took the stage. As they started to speak, one of my fellow spinners leaned over and whispered to me, "That's so-and-so. They're wonderful. They spin at the studio sometimes. They were originally involved with the *Chicken Soup for the Soul* series."
Whoa. Back up. What?

Say what you will about the *Chicken Soup for the Soul* series, the book was a *revolution*. The first of its kind—a collection of stories that was read *beyond* a high school Classic American Lit classroom (where most short story collections go to die). The first of its kind to break the mold. The first collection of stories to go mainstream and stay there.

I remember reading my first copy standing behind the counter working at the neighborhood video rental store (which has since become a liquor store). For me, that book was *hope. Proof.* People love stories. People will *buy* stories.

And there they were, standing on a stage within sight, two of the people who had made it happen. I wanted more than anything to bid on the painting they were auctioning off at that moment just to have a reason to cross the stage and shake their hands (when the painting sold for eleven thousand dollars, I was glad I had restrained myself). I hoped I might be able to catch them in the crowd afterward, to introduce myself, to thank them for their work, to maybe tell them a story of my own. But, after the final applause, the hugs goodbye, and the valet boy pulling the car around, I knew my opportunity to meet the legends, my heroes, had passed.

Unless....

That night at home, I told Michael about the *Chicken Soup* couple—how they were there, how I hadn't been able to shake their hands, how I heard they sometimes go to the studio to spin. As always, he had advice for his wife. He recommended, should I run into them at the spin studio someday, to invite them out to lunch.

Ask them to lunch? Yes, treat them to lunch and re-spectfully listen to anything they happened to say.

I thought it was brilliant. Lunch. I would invite them to lunch. That is... if I ever saw them. I hadn't seen them in class before and I had no way of knowing—or at least no way that didn't make me look like a stalker—what time they usually went to spin.

And then there they were.

• • • • •

I felt my tongue tie itself in knots as they greeted the owner of the studio and the girls working behind the counter and went into the spin room to secure their bikes.

The next few minutes were a blur. I remember blabbering to the owner of the studio and the girl behind the counter about how they were my idols, how I wanted to be a writer, how I couldn't believe they were here, how I wished I could get their autograph. There, in the midst of my hysteria, the owner took my hand, walked me into the room with the bikes and plopped me in front of my personal superstars.

"This is Kindra. She writes stories. She wanted to meet you." And with that, it was my turn to speak.

"Hi. Hi. Hi. (Embarrassed grin, and a too-tight grip on the handshake). Hi. Yes. I'm Kindra. Hi. Hi. Yes."

They kindly said hello after which I knew I had to say something more. Just then I remembered what Michael had said.

"Lunch!" I blurted out. "I would like you to go to lunch! I will, go. Too. To lunch. With you. The three of us. Eating lunch."

They were smiling, because they were very nice people.

"We'd love to talk with you. We could grab coffee," said

the *Chicken Soup* woman. She was even nicer in person than in the inspirational collections.

"I like to write. I write. Sometimes. Stories. Like you. Well. No. Not about soup. Just stories. I would love to know more about your soup stories." (I coached myself, *slow down Kindra; speak slowly*). "Lunch. I. Could. Do. Lunch. We. Could. Have. Soup. At. Lunch."

Still smiling, she spoke. "That's great that you write. We could grab coffee sometime."

"Yes! Lunch."

Ugh. It was like I had Afternoon Meal Tourette's Syndrome. No matter what I did, or what they said, the only word that came out of my mouth was *Lunch*.

"Maybe we could get your information? Do you have a card?" The very kind woman nervously moved the conversation along.

"Yes!" This was good. I could give them my card, they would go to my blog, and they would read that I'm actually *quite* normal. There was just one problem. I didn't have a card. Crap.

Never one to get discouraged, and apparently never one too concerned with professionalism, I turned on my heels and raced out of the spin room back to the lobby where I muttered to myself *"business card business card business card."* I needed *something* that could pass as a business card. AHA! A Post-it! I ran to the front counter where they had a whole stack of them. Blue ones. Bright blue Post-its. I grabbed one of the small squares of paper and began scribbling down my information.

Name.
Phone.
Email.
Website.
Facebook.
Twitter.
Address.
More and more and more.

Anything I could squeeze on there that might help them remember me or find me in the future, I did. How they met me, who introduced us, where I first saw them, what spin classes I usually come to, what bike I usually ride. The information curled up and over every inch of that blue Post-it until it was simply a maze of smudgy black ink.

I took a deep breath, gripped my Post-it Business Card, and walked back into the room with the *Chicken Soup* couple. They were still sitting on their bikes, though I'm sure escaping had crossed their minds.

"Here is my card." I thrust the sad, cluttered Post-it into the *Soup* woman's hand. "I look forward to grabbing lunch." Ugh.

Then, as if to spare me, the instructor dimmed the lights. It was time for class to start. I spent the rest of that hour with exercise as an afterthought. Despite it not being the *smoothest* introduction, I began day-dreaming about what my future might hold. I had just found the answer, the Holy Grail to short stories. Today was the first day of the rest of my life!

After class I thanked the owner for introducing me to the couple, who must have slipped out of class a little early because, sadly, I didn't see them in the lobby afterward. The owner smiled, told me what wonderful people they were, and that maybe—since they were pretty busy—I should just make it easy for them and grab *coffee* instead of lunch.

Ugh.

I called Michael as I pulled out of the parking lot to head home, sweaty and defeated. I told him I saw the *Chicken Soup* people, told him I talked to them, told him I gave them my number. Just as he was about to congratulate me, proud that I took a risk, I told him how I assaulted them with my incessant lunch invitations, told him about the overzealous Post-it, told him how the couple ran out before class had even ended. I could hear Michael shaking his head on the other end of the line.

I hung up the phone, and too embarrassed to be alone, I called someone else.

My dad answered.

The moment I said the words "You'll never guess who I just met," I could do no wrong. He hung on every word. It was exactly what I needed.

Apparently the ability to make a fool of yourself in front of celebrities is genetic. Perhaps that is my destiny. But perhaps that isn't always a bad thing.... Because a few months later I found myself, sitting at Starbucks, talking stories with the *Chicken Soup* people. And when I handed them a *real* business card, with only my necessary information on it, they gave me *back* my Post-it. Its job was done.

THE SECOND HONEYMOON

It was early June when Michael and I escaped the desert and fled to the Outer Banks of North Carolina. We had flown from Phoenix to Raleigh, stayed the night, driven five hours the next day to catch a ferry, and lost phone service somewhere during the forty-five-minute ride to the quaint-rustic-peaceful island of Ocracoke, North Carolina.

It had been a long day of travel in a miniature Ford Focus. Michael's navigator (who shall remain nameless) missed the only exit that had a Starbucks, thereby forcing Michael to function without coffee. Not ideal. Only *my* iPhone seemed to be compatible with the auxiliary radio device connection, which meant endless hours of music only one of us liked, which made it miserable for both of us. And every time we opened the door of the air-conditioned car, the windshield fogged from the humidity outside.

As our weary souls unloaded onto the island, we made our way to the beach house we would call home for the next week. We drove around the bay, past the surf shops and sweet shops and ice cream shops and Blackbeard Memorabilia shops. We rounded the corner where, between the tall sea grass and surrounded by multi-storied beach houses on stilts, we found a quaint little cottage. It was pink. It was tiny. It was perfect.

One word flashed through my mind:

SECONDHONEYMOON!

Second Honeymoon! Second Honeymoon! Second Honeymoon! The cottage was small with a pink door and a screened-in porch. It had a small seating area out front and an outdoor shower in the back. Before we even walked inside, suitcase in hand, I had visions of us sitting in the front, drinking wine until one of us gave the other "the look" and we slipped 'round back to 'cool off.' Inside there were two bedrooms, one with two twin beds for kids-or-suitcases, and one with a big bed for all of the passionate lovemaking.

We had a whole week of this paradise. What couple, after celebrating their first year of marriage, doesn't wish for a romantic escape to reconnect? And here we were! To be honest, we weren't expecting it—I was actually going to a storytelling workshop on the island with my favorite storyteller Donald Davis, and Michael was along to practice the art of doing absolutely nothing.

But *now* that it was a second honeymoon, in the hours where I wasn't in the workshop and Michael wasn't busy doing nothing, it would be all ROMANCE. We could take long walks on the beach, enjoy romantic dinners, and make passionate love all night.

Unfortunately, the first night was a challenging one. After meeting the other workshop goers for dinner, a late night folk music concert and one too many glasses of wine, Michael and I walked a mile home in the dark with only the moon, the fireflies and our iPhone "Flashlight" apps to guide us. Though I had hoped to start the Second Honeymoon that evening, it would have to wait until morning as we collapsed in bed and fell sound asleep. Clothes on.

The next several days can be characterized by a handful of things.

Humidity. We developed a whole new appreciation for the "Dry Heat."

Showers. Lots and Lots of solo-showers.

Bug Bites. More like battle wounds.

Fried Food. Fried scallops, fried oysters, fried fish, fried pickles, fried-you-name-it-I-ate-it.

Ice Cream. To combat the humidity. I had at least two cones a day.

Sweet Shop. Homemade fudge. I tried every flavor.

Coffee Shop. Homemade cinnamon rolls.

Pizza. I. Love. Pizza.

Workshops and Doing Nothing.

Sex. Well... not exactly.

• • • • •

As the week wore on, I found the clothing I brought to be unsatisfactory. Not only because any clothing at all was too hot *(I longed to go back to the days when I was little and my mother would lay a sheet in the middle of the living room floor, under the ceiling fan, in our un-air-conditioned house, and I would lay there in my panties and watch Charlotte's Web until the summer was over)*, but because the clothing items were getting increasingly smaller. I thought it must be the oppressive humidity that was forcing my insides, including the insides of my thighs, to swell in protest. Though when I Googled "Humidity and Immediate Swelling that Makes Your Clothes Not Fit," I got even less satisfactory results. Then I thought I must be pregnant. People gain weight when they're pregnant. Maybe I was like one of those women on TV who didn't know she was pregnant until the baby came out in the bathroom. Sure I was on the pill, and sure I showed no signs of creating a human, but it *was* possible. None of the other toiletmothers showed signs.

I would stand in the little beach cottage bathroom and study my bulges in the mirror. There were definitely lumps that weren't there before my secondhoneymoon, that weren't there on my first honeymoon. I asked Michael if I looked fat. I asked if that lump was there a few days ago. I told him I thought I was pregnant and asked if he was ready to be a father to a bathroom baby. He didn't answer. I figured he was still busy doing nothing and didn't want to be interrupted.

In the days to come, as we walked around the island, sweating and scratching the prehistoric-sized chomps out of our skin, I talked more about my fatness. How much I hated feeling chubby. How much I wished I could just be one of those skinny people. And as we walked by another ice cream shop, I dragged him in and he watched me eat them dry of Peppermint Bon-Bon.

At night, after the fireflies and the fourth shower of the day, we lay side.by.side in bed with a world between us. There in the dark, I would ask him the worst question of all, my greatest fear.

"Are you not having sex with me because I'm fat and unattractive?"

I would drift off to sleep before I heard the answer; before a kiss goodnight.

· · · · ·

As our second honeymoon dragged on, I could feel him pulling away from me and though I *always* talked more than he did, I could tell he was unusually silent. I knew it was probably because he had something big to say that was blocking everything else from coming out. And I knew I wouldn't like it.

On the sixth evening of what would now be called the SEXLESSHONEYMOON, we walked home among the fireflies, thoroughly annihilated the bugs that had crept in the house with hopes of devouring us, and enjoyed a glass of wine on the screened-in porch. I was determined to create an environment where Michael felt free to speak. I prepared myself for what those words might be and I crossed and uncrossed my legs (because I was nervous and also because they had gotten too big to stay crossed on their own for longer than a minute or two). We fell into easy, comfortable Kindra-Michael conversation and the world felt right once again. Before long we slipped into the bedroom, crawled in the bed, and it wasn't until we were under the covers that he spoke the words he had been holding back.

"Kindra, do you remember our vows?"
Oh this was never a good way for a conversation to start.
Yes. I remember them.
"Do you remember the line we wrote that said: 'I promise to live a healthy life that our days together may be plenty?"
Yes. I remember that line.
"Do you remember *why* we wrote it?"
Yes....
His next words were said with love, hurt, concern and a little bit of man.

Kindra. I don't know what to say to you when you ask me if you're fat. I don't know what to do when you stand in front of the mirror pushing, poking, and frowning at yourself. Worst of all, I don't know how to stop you from making the choices that get you there. What should I say when you insist on another ice cream cone and I know it will make you hate yourself later. I know you know better. I know we're on "vacation" and I know you're supposed to relax with eating when you're on "vacation"... but how can either of us relax at all when you're so mad at yourself you can't talk about anything but how lumpy you are? Who wants to have sex with someone who feels that way about themselves? Kindra, I don't want to get to a point where we can't call each other out on our unhealthy choices. I've seen it happen, and it isn't pretty. It's dangerous. Small bad choices are a slippery slope. So I'm telling you now. You know how to make healthy choices... and if you can't do it for me, do it so you will like yourself better.

Whoa.

The man was brave.

On our wedding day we promised to live a healthy life—exercise, good food choices, wearing our seat belts, calling a cab after a night out, and on and on. I knew I wasn't being healthy and I was frustrated with myself;

what woman isn't frustrated when she puts on a pair of running shorts that she loved a few months ago (and paid *way* too much for) and now they make her thighs chafe. I realized how those choices were affecting me.... I hadn't considered how they were affecting Michael, except to shallowly believe that it was just a sex deterrent.

There, in the dark and humid room, I had little more to say than I'm sorry. I'm sorry, and thank you. I made a promise to him, and to myself, to make better choices, to make the choices we *both* deserved.

We were both so exhausted from the discussion, with a hug and a kiss, we fell asleep. Content.

The next morning, my period arrived.

And since we're not the kind of couple who does *that*, any hope for a sex-filled SECONDHONEYMOON were over. Two days later, we went home.

• • • • •

I could call it The Second Honeymoon That Never Was, but that wouldn't be true. Though we never stopped sweating, though I still get a little nauseous when I think of fried oysters (apparently you're not supposed to *look* at them), though I have scars on my legs from the dinosaur insects that bit me, and though we went ten days with absolutely no sex....

There is simply nothing sexier than the overwhelming romance of honesty.

MARTA VON TRAPP

Sixth grade was not a good year for me.

It was my first year of middle school. My homeroom teacher never combed her hair and she reminded me of the cardboard witch we hung in our kitchen window at Halloween. My Language Arts teacher, who was hired mainly for her gymnastics coaching ability, taught us that more than one monkey was "monkies" and that the 'there-their-they're' mystery was more hype than reality. I *did* love my math teacher, Mr. Sauerbry, and loved my science teacher Mr. Tengwall (until he dropped a minnow in a vat of dry ice to show us just how cold it really was and then snapped the minnow in half for demonstration). I was taunted in gym class when we

played anything involving a ball and longed for the days
of shaking the big parachute then hiding underneath
it. In sixth grade I was still recovering from a really bad
haircut two years before. I hadn't updated my elemen-
tary apparel to appropriate junior high fashion. I was
too embarrassed to wear a training bra even though I
needed one. While other girls were reading *YM* magazine, I was still happy with my subscription to *Disney
Adventures*. Somehow, my locker ended up on the third
floor with all the seventh graders instead of in the
basement with the other sixth graders and the seventh
graders frequently launched attacks on the intruder. Me.
The intruder. The kids at the bus stop threw rocks at
me, and looking back, I'm not sure I had real friends.

From the first day I knew it was going to be a long year.

And then, as if by miracle, I was cast in a neighboring
school district's high school play—*The Sound of Music*.

I was Marta von Trapp. And it saved my life.

While junior high kids seemed to despise me, the high
school kids playing nuns, Nazis, and a traveling, singing
troupe of siblings seemed to *adore* me. They talked to
me. They laughed with me. They encouraged me. They

wanted to be my friends. During the course of those few months I felt like myself again. I could be silly and creative and wear ugly clothes and no one seemed to care. In a time where I almost lost myself, somewhere in the hills alive with music, I was safe.

The show ran for two weekends, and on the last night I dreamed that the curtains would malfunction, making them impossible to close—that the show would go on. Forever. That I could skip sixth grade. That I could be Marta for the rest of my life.

That last night I was invited to the Closing Night Cast Party at one of the nun's houses. Despite the fact that I was only eleven, my mother and father allowed their daughter to go to a party with the high school kids who made her so happy. It was a chilly fall night. We, the Von Trapp family, nuns, and Nazis alike, went on a hayride through the fields and forest behind the rural home. We sat in the basement, drank cider and hot chocolate with marshmallows, and ate Cool Ranch Doritos and pizza. We were all hanging out, sharing stories from the show, when the girl who played Louisa von Trapp (my singing-sibling) took me by the hand and brought me out into the yard in front of the house.

There the full moon cut through the tall pines so that, in between the shadows, it looked like daylight. Louisa had been one of my favorites in the whole play. She was tall and thin with long, golden blond hair and bright blue eyes. Her face was innocent, like a Cabbage Patch doll that shed her baby-fat and now could sing and dance and drive a car. We sat in the grass for a bit. We talked about silly things I don't remember. And then Louisa asked me if I wanted to try something cool.

With all the trust in the world, I said yes. Louisa didn't disappoint.

She told me to get on my hands and knees. I did. I could see my breath as it froze in the space between my lips and the ground. She told me to close my eyes. I did. She told me to feel the Earth in my hands below me. I could; it was cold and hard and wet and prickly. It was getting ready for winter—for the first snow that would come only a few days later, erasing any evidence that we had been there. Then Lousia told me to imagine that instead of just kneeling there on the grass, a bystander on the Earth, that I was actually *holding* it. That as this incredible mass rocketed through the universe, it was actually in the palm of my hand. She told me to imagine that at this moment, on this piece of Earth, I was holding the world up. After a moment of silence and wonder, I opened my eyes with my hands firmly entangled in the grass, holding on for dear life. The world had never looked so new.

Louisa spoke softly then, as if to herself, as if she knew the pain of being eleven, being in sixth grade, of not wanting to wear a training bra and of the cruelty of other children. As if she knew that beyond sixth grade, the world can be tough. On all fours herself, she whispered that when the world was getting the best of you all you had to do was take a moment to hold it in the palm of your hands. That's how you know you still have a place. That even if it's just this one piece of land where your hands and knees are planted, there is a place for you.

And the possibilities for you are infinite.

I wasn't sure if it was the moonlight or the dampness of the nighttime air, but as Louisa and I walked back into the house hand in hand, both our eyes glistened.

• • • • •

If you ever need a reminder of these things; that you have a place, that your possibilities are infinite, take a moment, slip outside, feel the Earth between your fingers, and the world in the palm of your hands.

THE ROAD LESS TRAVELED

I have a flaw.

I *love* revenge.

Not violent revenge... no. I enjoy revenge of a different
kind. I love the thrill of getting someone back using
nothing but the strength of my mind and the power of
my wit. I smile as I imagine the conversation with my
opponent—my verbal jabs and their feeble responses.
I wait for the perfect moment to clobber them with my
words.
Fortunately (or unfortunately), in the era of online social
networking, there is *always* a perfect time.
Because the Internet never sleeps.

• • • • •

I remember my first experience with online revenge. In 2006 I was involved in an unsolicited MySpace WAR. I was attacked by my ex-boyfriend's new girlfriend and her posse of minions. We quarreled back and forth with some meaningless taunts and then they turned ugly. I was armed with a truckload of verbal bombs and was just about to drop them on the foolish girls' Internet world when my mom called.

I told her about the battle, told her what I planned to do, and though she barely knew what the Internet *was* at the time, much less MySpace, she strongly advised against it. She gave me the whole "don't sink to their level/ignore them and they'll go away/if you don't have something nice to say" line of crap she'd been giving me since I was a child.

She told me to take the high road.

And just like when I was a child, I knew she was right. Argh! I was so mad. I was *so* looking forward to my revenge.
That night, I signed into MySpace. I didn't post any comments. I didn't change any statuses.

I *did* however, post a MySpace *blog*.

No one said *anything* about abstaining from vengeful MySpace *blogging*. Besides, I had decided to take the high road—this was just my farewell note to the losers traveling lowly.

Thirty minutes, a few smirks and a smile later, I posted this:

It is an interesting thing. You can go to the store, and purchase a map, and the map will show you everything you need to know about your chosen city: the streets, the freeways, the parks, and other various attractions. Despite the fact that it is almost impossible to fold the map back up again when you are finished (we actually spent an entire class period on map-folding in sixth grade social studies), for the most part a map is a very good thing to have.

But have you ever had an experience with your map where you could not find the road someone was telling you to take? Spent long periods of time staring at the map, trying to find the road, checking the "see inset" box, examining the creases where the map had been folded incorrectly, and yet the road is still nowhere to be found?

*Ah yes, that's because you're looking for the very elusive—
High road.*

*Oh, you have heard of the "high road"; you may have
even seen it from a distance. Your friends or family may
have told you to take the high road during a particularly
vile situation, when perhaps you were planning (plotting,
scheming) something different. But on more than one
occasion, you didn't take their direction.... On more than
one occasion you probably took a different route....*

*The question is, Why? Why didn't you take the high road
when you probably should have? It's not because of
the traffic; the high road is usually pretty open. It is not
because it is dangerous: It's about the safest route you
can take.*

The fact of the matter is, the high road sucks.

*The high road is a miserable bore; people falling asleep at
the wheel of their unsatisfied revenge. This is why it's so
difficult to locate on a map; instead of a bustling freeway,
it is often not much more than an overgrown path (and not
the picturesque kind). There may, however, be a solution—
a way to make the high road more interesting for those of
us who prefer a little excitement in our travels.*

Perhaps if someone were to post interesting, entertaining, or encouraging billboards along the high road, it would make the ride more enjoyable. Billboards that reminded those who travel the high road:

"No doubt about it, you're way better."
"What is wrong with her face?"
"You make SO much more money."
"Feel bad for people who are boring—and be happy you're not one of them."
"You are DEFINITELY better in bed."

Maybe the signs light up, or are very colorful. Maybe there is a shop at the beginning of the high road where you can customize your own sign, perfectly suited to your vile situation which you have now left behind.... T-shirts, bumper stickers, kitschy key chains.

But alas, the truth is... it doesn't really matter. The only thing that makes the high road remotely satisfying is the moment when you get to say to your opponent, "I am taking the high road," thus pointing out their pathetic state. Unfortunately, as soon as you SAY you're taking the high road, you are immediately exiting off of it.

By default, taking the high road must be done anony-

mously—the final unsatisfying reality of this noble path.

That being said, I am anonymously hitting the high road. I have filled my tank, I have my map ready, and I will reach my destination with much more dignity than "some" people.

So long, and may your travels be fulfilling no matter which road you take.

My blog had more traffic in the twenty-four hours following that post than it had ever seen.

Ahh sweet revenge.

· · · · ·

The world of status updates and tweets is a dangerous place for those of us who enjoy a little verbal revenge from time to time. Since 2006, I have made it a habit to keep all of my beautifully crafted, vengeful online statements, whether about politics, a person, or their posse of minions, to myself. I believe this is what my mother would recommend if she knew how Facebook worked. And she'd be right.

While the satisfaction from a sassy status update is *real*, sadly, it is fleeting. By the same time tomorrow, a vengeful status update will line the trash cans of yesterday's newsfeed and you'll be left feeling a little worse for it.

So though the high road is dull, I've decided to do my best to follow it and take as few exits as possible. After all, it *is* the fastest route to success... and *success* is the sweetest revenge of all.

MANIFESTING

My brother's life sucked.

It really did, he assured me. His was a crappy, crappy life and it was getting worse.

He had just finished college with a degree in film. In school he had received many accolades for his works—a prodigy of sorts. And while he hadn't necessarily expected instant Spielberg-like fame, he *had* expected *something* to happen. He bought a book filled with people to send his work to, he reached out to a few personal contacts, and he watched the web for any opportunities that could launch his film career into hyper-stardom. The result? Nothing. Absolutely nothing. This meant the film prodigy was working the graveyard shift in the stock room at the local Target by night, living in my parents' basement by day, and during every minute of all of it he loathed what his life had become.

I sat on the other end of the phone as he painted the pathetic picture of his future. As an older sister and one to always look for the silver lining, I tried to point out the good in his situation—he still had his talent and he didn't have an exciting social life to distract him. But each of my linings was shredded instantly with his words of utter hopelessness and his unwillingness to see anything except what was going wrong. I stayed cool as long as I could, but finally I couldn't take any more of his "my life sucks/why me" attitude.

"PATRICK!" I said into the phone with more force than I had hoped. "PATRICK, *please*, for a minute, LOOK AT WHAT YOU'RE MANIFESTING!"

Oh yes, *The Secret* had just been released (I had watched it just enough to not see its many flaws) and I knew the universe was singing his ugly, ugly song. I also knew the only way he would be able to break the downward spiral of negativity would be to change his thoughts. But by default older sisters sound preachy, so instead of a lecture, I told him this story.

• • • • •

There was a time when I traveled a fair amount for work. And as it turned out, since we worked together, Michael often came with me; we were kind of a two-man show, touring the country, giving presentations. I loved it. Loved cruising expertly through airport security. Loved settling into my seat on the plane. Loved touching down in a new city. Loved finding our way to the hotel and grabbing a bite to eat before things got hectic. We went from city to city with our laptops and a week's worth of professional apparel that spanned the temperatures of the West Coast, then Chicago, then Denver in February, all meticulously placed in an overhead-appropriate bag.

One of my favorite stops was of course San Francisco. Unfortunately, one foul afternoon this fair city became a place of pain and suffering.

It was May. We arrived with our two carry-on roller bags at the Comfort Inn by the Bay in San Francisco at 4 p.m. We had been there before. Like old pros we approached the front desk and executed the whole "check-in at the hotel" ballet flawlessly. However, in the arrival whirlwind there *was* a moment's pause; it was the moment in which I reached down to pick my laptop bag off the ground. In the weeks and months to come, I replayed that moment in slow motion in my mind....

As I bent over, moved my hair from on

e s h o u l d e r to the o t h e r, g r a b b e d my l
a p t o p, a n d b e g a n to s t a n d s t r a i g h t...
m y e y e s f e l l u p o n a s m a l l s i g n t h a t r e
a d:

Pardon our mess. We are in the midst of minor renova-
tions. This should not interfere with your stay. Enjoy
your time at the Comfort Inn by the Bay.

I b l i n k e d o n c e, t u r n e d o n m y h e e l s, a n
d h e a d e d t o w a r d t h e e l e v a t o r a n d o u
r s e v e n t h f l o o r, G o l d e n – G a t e – V i e w h o
m e f o r t h e n e x t t w o n i g h t s.

The sign was so nonchalant I thought little of it as we
quickly changed and headed back out to our first work
engagement. I thought little of it as we arrived later that
evening after a successful taking-over-the-world presentation and collapsed into bed. I thought little of it as we
shuffled our way downstairs for a luxurious breakfast of
continental hard-boiled eggs, various toast-able breads,
and pastries that are no better than the ones you find at
the corner gas station. In fact, the sign didn't cross my
mind until we got back up to our floor, stood outside our
room, and from the hallway we heard The Noise.

It sounded like a trip to the dentist; if the dentist had a drill that could reach the seventh floor of a hotel and if you had teeth the size of a window facing the Golden Gate Bridge.

As we opened the door a strange shadow was cast across our entire room—the shadow of three men on an airborne platform wearing goggles, masks, and high-powered ear covers. All three of them were hanging on to a single device that resembled a jackhammer and were jamming it into the spaces between our window frame and the brick.

It was *THEN* that the sign crossed my mind....
And I was furious.
What kind of cruel understating moron made that sign?

Unfortunately for us, the hotel did not provide high-powered ear covers to their guests. The drilling sound was brain-scrambling, and I found myself paralyzed where I stood. Michael could tell I was about to scream, which would only add to his misery, and in an effort to maintain some semblance of control, he grabbed my sunglasses, took my hand, and led me back to the door, back to the hallway, back to the elevator, and out to the street.

"It's a beautiful day in San Francisco," (clouds, chill, a little rain). "No reason we should spend it inside," he said. And so began our impromptu sightseeing tour. We walked to the wharf, bought some cheap sunglasses, ate some soup out of a bread bowl, looked at the seals, and were asked if we had any spare change no fewer than fifteen times. After two hours of strolling the streets and lunch at a restaurant where we decided only tourists went (because no one would ever go there twice), we figured it was safe for us to return to the hotel room— that the dinosaur dentist had likely moved on to another victim. After all, we had work to complete and primping to do before our presentation that evening.

While I would like to say that when we returned to our room The Noise had ceased, that would be a lie. For the next two hours we sat in the room with the curtains closed (since strange men were hanging right outside our window) and Michael watched TV, seemingly un-fazed by the horror of it all. I, on the other hand, went crazy. I hid under my pillow, I turned on my iPod, I paced the room, I tried screaming louder than the drill, "my life sucks/why me," and eventually I took a show-er—washing, rinsing, and repeating the sound away.

When I *finally* removed myself from the water-and-steam

cocoon, I was officially running late. From the shower
I hurried to the mirror to commence the "get-ready-
as-fast-as-you-can-dance"; a dance Michael fears—as
tragedy is typically the grand finale.

What a tragedy it was.

Obviously shaken by the inescapable noise and rushed
pace, my hair wouldn't dry, straighten, OR curl. A closer
look at my eyes revealed a bloodshot garden of stress
which I tried to remedy with a splash of ClearEyes—a
good plan until I dropped the dripper, point down,
onto the bar of cheap hotel soap. That meant a chunk
of generic cleansing bar lodged itself in the ClearEyes
applicator, which I then shot straight into my cornea. I
stumbled back, soap burning in the depths of my eye,
eyelid squeezed shut against future attacks, screaming
in extremely overdramatic agony.

My life sucked. *This sucks, this sucks, why me, why me*
I repeated as I tossed on some eyeliner and mascara,
which streaked down my cheeks while I moved to the
hotel iron and ironing board. Window-drilling in the
background, eye still sealed shut, I stood in my bra and
panties and furiously pressed my slacks and top.

Whether it was my compromised vision, my exaggerated high-speed motion, or my disorientation from the incessant drilling that caused what happened next, I'm not entirely sure. But what I *am* sure of is that *one* moment I was ironing and the *next* moment I had stopped....

I seemed to be unable to locate the iron. I knew it was in my hand, but I didn't see its usual back and forth motion on the board. In fact, for some reason, it. felt. stuck.

I stood there, shirt on the ironing board, iron scorching the skin on my stomach for what had to have been a full minute before I realized what was happening. When the "You are burning your stomach" message finally arrived at my brain, I screamed in *more* agony as I peeled away the deviant appliance. I threw the iron on the board, clutched the three-inch-long blistered mess on my abdomen, and collapsed backward on the bed behind me.

MY LIFE SUCKS. WHY ME.

I screamed so loud the drilling actually stopped.

Michael raced from the shower to see what had happened. In a flash-assessment of the situation, he first removed the iron from resting atop my shirt on the ironing board, then soaked a towel in cold water to apply to my wound. While I wailed, he finished ironing my clothes. I hollered as he helped me crawl into them, and when I wouldn't stop screaming he grabbed me by the shoulders and shook me.

"LOOK AT WHAT YOU'RE MANIFESTING."

I stopped screaming.

Michael wasn't usually a yeller but here his words were harsh and his expression was exasperated and thoroughly annoyed. I wanted to yell back, but it was clear he was resolved in his analysis of the situation. And even though *The Secret* was *way* over-quoted and kind of annoying…. He was right. Ever since I had seen that fateful sign in the lobby, my subconscious (and then my conscious) was sending nothing but negative wavelengths into the universe… and I was getting nothing but negative back.

I scraped the smeared mascara from my face, applied some lotion to the wound and we left the hotel for another meeting where we planned to take over the world.

• • • • •

I shared this story with my brother, not because the situations were the same—clearly they were quite different—but rather because I remembered a day when my life sucked and everything kept getting worse. And I remembered how Michael's words seemed harsh at first, but if he hadn't been brave enough to snap me out of it, who knows how long it would have lasted. It doesn't take much for a bad day to become a bad week, a bad month, a bad year, a wasted lifetime. I knew my brother was better than that—what I *didn't* know was if he had someone in his life to say so.

I didn't hear from Patrick for a while after that. Years later he admitted that he thought my theory was dumb—that I had joined some sort of New Age cult. But he also figured he had nothing to lose. "Be miserable and think miserably, or be miserable and think positively?" So he started fabricating positive thoughts as a pastime to fill the long hours in the stockroom. Then a strange thing happened; almost immediately after thinking repetitively and with little faith that "my life will be awesome," awesome things began to happen. Now, years later living in his *own* apartment, he impresses the masses with his video skills—the graveyard stockroom days a distant memory. And though the scar on my abdomen from my battle with The Day That Kept

Getting Worse has long since faded, the memory of that day *did* leave its mark; one random afternoon Patrick informed me that it was the "Manifesting Story" that snapped him out of his negative haze and set him on a better path. And he wanted to thank me.

As an older sister, I don't think I've ever been more proud.

A STINT AS SPIELBERG

One night, over dinner, Michael and I decided we should be wedding videographers. It seemed like the perfect idea. We had a camera. We had Macs. And we saw how much money even the crappy wedding videographers made for a Saturday afternoon of work. That was all the motivation we needed.

Our business plan was simple. Film the wedding. Edit the wedding. Make lots of money on the weekends. Simple. As far as we could tell, there were only two problems:

1. We needed a wedding to video-graph and
2. I was incapable of pronouncing the word videographer

any other way than "video-ographer"

Though we have yet to solve the second problem, we found a solution for the first.

Joni.

Joni was one of my best friends from college and Joni was getting married. This was particularly exciting because Joni loved weddings more than anyone. ever. in the history of brides, weddings, and happily-ever-afters. Joni had a stack of wedding magazines sitting on the floor of our college house bathroom. Every morning she sat on the toilet and turned each one of the four hundred pages of advertisements with a delicate hand and a wistful gaze. When we heard noises coming from the bathroom, they were usually dreamy sighs from Joni as she wondered, with her panties around her ankles, what her Day might bring.

Finally her day had come.

And so had ours.

Joni would be the first client of "Michael and Kindra Now Do Wedding Videos" (our temporary company name).

Because she wasn't sure she wanted a videographer at all, we gave her a price she couldn't refuse. Free. We chalked it up to portfolio-building. And even though I was a bridesmaid with a myriad of other responsibilities, we were determined.

The day came and went with few disasters, video or otherwise. Because I was a part of the wedding, we were able to capture footage that other videographers could not, including the rehearsal dinner after party where a random drunk woman wet her pants and wouldn't put down the tambourine. It was unfortunate that the pastor had forgotten to turn on his microphone, so we had no sound at the ceremony, and unfortunate that Michael only videoed the friends he knew at the reception (all five of them) so it looked like attendance was low. However, overall, we were pleased with the footage and were excited to go home and make a masterpiece.

We were, after all, videographers.

In fact, we were videographers for the entire year.
Twelve months exactly.
Did we film more weddings? No.

Did we find new clients? No.
We spent the next year editing Joni's wedding video.
All. Year. Long.

On the 364th day of the project, we finally finished. We wrapped up several copies and sent them overnight Saturday delivery to the (no longer a) newlywed Joni. Joni saw her wedding video for the first time on her one-year anniversary with her husband and three-month-old son.

Yes. Joni was able to conceive, grow, and birth a child in the amount of time it took us to put music to a total of twenty minutes of edited film.

I did not ask for a customer review.

I learned several things from this experience.

First, wedding videographers should charge more.
If each wedding takes a year to edit, the hourly rate breakdown is not ideal. It would be difficult to feed a fish with that income, much less a family.

Second, I'm not very good at video-ography. I have a shaky hand in the taping stage and I get a little carried away with the special effects in editing.... It's like I can make the real world look like a dream! (The mantra of all crappy videographers.)

Third, and most important: Just because you *can* do something doesn't mean you *should*. We are all more gifted in some areas than in others. Time spent doing the things you "*can*" do is time stolen from the things you were *born* to do.

Michael and I have officially closed the door on our wedding videography business—so please, resist the temptation to hire us. When it comes to weddings, I am going to stick to what I do best: dancing the night away.

COMING CLEAN

I was in the middle of an intense conversation with my girlfriend, Alex. I had some concerns, real concerns, concerns that I needed to share with someone if for no other reason than to hear them nod and sigh with approval on the other end of the line. About twenty minutes into the conversation, I reached the *height* of my concerns.

Kaboom.

I waited. Waited for a response. Waited for a GASP. Or a NO WAY KINDRA. Waited for *anything* really. And when she didn't respond after a few seconds, I talked for another minute, making sure she correctly understood the situation so that she could properly respond.

Still silent.

With some trepidation I said her name and then pulled
the phone away from my face.
The screen was dark. Very dark.
The battery had apparently had enough of my overly
dramatic account of the day's events and my phone had
turned itself off.
At what *point* had it turned itself off? I wasn't sure. All
I knew is that, for however long, I had been Talking. to.
Myself.

Something about that is SO embarrassing.

Which is weird ... because, by default, the other person
doesn't know you did it.
Right?
Because they are *no longer on the other end of the phone.*
Which is the very *reason* you are *talking to yourself.*

If a tree falls in the forest and no one is there to see it...
should it be embarrassed it was so clumsy?

Nevertheless, I am always mortified. And the very first

thing I do when I get the other person back on the line is tell them how long I talked and talked and talked before I realized they weren't there. I tell them how stupid I must have looked and how embarrassed I am that it happened.

I don't know... there's something about coming clean that makes it better.

Which is why I'm going to tell you what I'm going to tell you next.
I'm hoping coming clean will make me better.

• • • • •

It was a Saturday afternoon and I was going to make a purchase. I had had my eye on a white lawn chair that would be perfect for sunning myself in the approaching Arizona spring. I had hoped Michael would buy it *for* me, but he said no. No, because if I wanted a chair, I had to buy it with my *own* money. Yes. We have separate bank accounts for purchases just like this—things we would individually like to buy without having to ask permission and without running the risk of reprimand or judgment. But I never like spending the money in my personal bank account. I like to watch it sit there and pile up as I twiddle my fingers together wondering what extravagant thing I could buy....

A white plastic chair was not extravagant, but nevertheless I wanted it.

That Saturday I purchased my chair and when the little
scanner machine asked if I wanted cash back, I got a
little wild. I took out forty WHOLE dollars from my personal account. Two twenty-dollar bills that I told myself
I could spend in *wild* ways. I was giddy as I considered
the possibilities. I felt like a little girl who just pounded
her piggybank open with a hammer and was now stuff-
ing the shiny coins in her Rainbow Brite purse.

I put the two twenties in my wallet, grabbed my chair,
and headed home... victorious.

The day passed with little excitement, and as the
evening approached I still had not thought of a worthy-
enough way to spend my precious twenties. Also, with
the approaching sunset came a text message; an invitation from some new friends to attend church with them
in the morning. Michael had made other plans and I
initially refused the offer (because I was planning to go
to spin and because I'm not a regular churchgoer and
had just gone the week before and two weeks in a row

seemed like a lot), but changed my mind when I awoke Sunday morning.

I sent a text to my new friends letting them know I'd be there and to save a seat with them in the second row right behind the pastors. I quickly got ready, hopped in my car and drove the twenty-five minutes to church.

I was about halfway there when I realized something... realized I had *forgotten* something.

An offering. I hadn't brought an offering.
Oh crap.

I had only been to this church once with my new friends before but I *knew* that at some point early on they were going to pass around buckets and everybody was going to throw their money in. I *knew* that I would be standing there, with my new friends, and they would see me *NOT* put any money in the bucket. And even though we were at church, and even though church is the one place where people shouldn't be judged, and even though Michael *did* put money in the bucket the last time we were there, which would mean we were fifty-fifty on offerings, which is still not too bad, I *knew* I would be known as the girl who sat in the second row right behind the pastors and didn't give an offering.

I also *knew*....
But didn't want to admit....

That I DID have an offering.
The forty dollars in my wallet from the day before.
Cash.
Two twenty-dollar bills.
Two twenties I had requested when I bought my chair.
Two twenties I planned to spend....
Selfishly.
Wildly.
They were my two *wild, selfish* twenty-dollar bills that I
could spend any way I wanted....
And throwing one of them in a bucket with a bunch of
other people's money at church was neither wild nor
selfish.

More important than social pressure, more important
than being judged for my lack of charity, I simply did not
want to have to separate from my twenty-dollar bills. At
least, not without a pair of shoes or a cute top to show
for it.

I would simply have to think of something else.

The worship band was just getting started when I made my way to my saved seat in the second row of the enormous auditorium. I hugged my friends, I smiled at the pastors in front of me, and I clapped along as I read the words to the worship songs on the Jumbotron screens.

Yet, through all the singing, all the hand-clapping, all the good feelings... through it all, I was crafting the story I would tell when the bucket passing commenced and the pail came my way. I carefully rehearsed what I would do when the bucket passed from me to the next without any additional tithe. By the end of the second song, after much thought and consideration (and little praise to God) I had it....

I would simply lean over to my friend and whisper with great concern,
"Oh shoot! Michael is the one who carries the cash! I'm so embarrassed! I'll have to make up for it next time."

People have forgotten cash before, right?
Especially non-churchgoers like me.
And yes, even though I had two matching twenties in my wallet... that didn't mean I *had* to give them.
I mean, I was *there*, right? Isn't that good enough for God?

I waited for a response.

Waited for a You're Right Kindra.

Waited for a Sigh of Approval.

Waited for *anything.*

But everything was silent.

It was at that moment I realized... at some point during

the crafting and telling of my twisted tale, the battery

that fuels my conscience....

Died.

No one was listening to my nonsense anymore.

I was left stuttering and stammering and without the

approval I was seeking, and no one was on the other end

of the line.

And even though no one knew....

I was SO embarrassed.

I couldn't believe I was going to *lie.*

Lie to friends who I had just met.

Lie to *myself.* I actually tried to convince *myself* that I

did not have cash when I was the one who had put it in

my wallet the day before.

Lie in *church*, of all places.

And for what? For twenty dollars?

There are people with a lot less than me who give a lot more—whether in church or elsewhere—without a second thought.

I was SO embarrassed. Embarrassed of my greedy, lying self.

It was the bucket that woke me from my haze. I was so deep in thought I nearly dropped it, spilling hard-earned ones, fives, tens, and twenties to the floor. Once I regained control I quickly reached for my wallet and grabbed one of the Wild Twenty Dollar Bills. I tossed it in with the others and passed the bucket to my right.

And it felt good.

Not the giving of the money, not the fact that I was "Giving to the Lord," not the implied selflessness of the act.... It just felt good to not be embarrassed of myself.

Maybe it's the wrong reason for giving an offering in church, but on that Sunday, it was good enough for me.

• • • • •

This is not a story about church. This is not a story about giving. This is not a story about money.

This is not even a story about the social pressures of tithing.

It's about coming clean in the hope that we become better.

This is a story that, if I had kept it to myself, no one would have known I fell in the woods. It happened in a flash on a Sunday morning and no one was there, on the inside, to see how it all came down. Keeping this story, this event to myself, I would have been spared the humiliation that comes when you reveal the ugly parts.

But we all do things—stupid twenty-dollar things—that are often unnoticed by others, but that are truly embarrassing.

Gossiping about friends.

White lies.

Quietly making fun of people as they pass.

Small cheatings of the system.

These are things that make us a little worse than we want to be, and we owe it to ourselves to do better than that.

Today, as embarrassing as it is, I am coming clean in the hope that we can *all* be a little bit less embarrassed of ourselves.

That we can be better.

· · · · ·

As for the other twenty-dollar bill....

The twenty dollars I had such high hopes for....

Yeah.

I have no idea what happened to that twenty dollars.

I think I spent some at the grocery store.

And probably some at Pita Jungle on a chicken schwarma.

THE DAY MY DAY WAS ALMOST RUINED

It happened about one week after moving into Michael's condo.

My day was almost ruined.

We had recently gotten engaged and, against my better judgment, decided we should move in together. His condo was an urban loft where the only separation between rooms was half walls. The only rooms with doors were the bathroom and the closet; difficult conditions under which to combine lives. Not only were we struggling with the normal challenges of personal space, the various definitions of clean, bathroom time, and how much walking-around-naked is too much ... we *also* had to discuss the appropriate volume for the television after one of us (me) retired to the bedroom of the wall-less condo while the other (he) fell asleep to Comedy Central. Finally, and perhaps most difficult of all, we had to decide if what's mine is *really* yours.

I've always been a "what's mine is mine unless I say otherwise" person, while Michael was more of a "what's yours is yours unless I want to eat it" kind of guy.

This subtle difference almost ruined my day.

• • • • •

One day, about a week after I had moved in, I woke up with the overwhelming urge to eat a bowl of TRIX cereal. It was so powerful, I had no choice but to drive to the grocery store in my PJs, pick up a red box with a floppy-eared rabbit on it, come home and pour a bowl *immediately*. It was *amazing*. I ate every last puff *and* polished off the pinkish milk before Michael had even stirred in his sleep.

That evening I went to bed early as usual, Michael stayed up as usual, and I fell asleep dreaming of TRIX for breakfast.

The next day, after a morning walk and while Michael

was in the shower, I was ready for another bowl of the childhood delicacy. I went to the fridge but noticed there was no milk. Odd. I went to the pantry and noticed there was no TRIX. Very odd. Slightly confused, I paused.

Where could they be?
It was then that a thought occurred to me. An *awful* thought.

I slowly walked to the garbage can.
There, both containers waited.
Empty. Used. Depleted.

I
was
FURIOUS.

I had enjoyed *one* bowl of cereal and then, while I *slept*, like a thief in the night, my so-called loving fiancé devoured the *entire* rest of the box.

I ran to the bathroom door and began pounding on it with both fists and yelling things like "TRIX ARE FOR KINDRAS!" and "I'M GOING TO EAT ALL OF THE SIRLOINS IN THE FREEZER WHILE YOU SLEEP!" and

"I THOUGHT YOU LOVED ME." I then collapsed on the bed and waited for him to emerge.

Shortly after, Michael walked out of the bathroom in a cloud of steam, and I. Was. Waiting. Ready to unleash the fury.

"What?" he asked (as if he didn't know).

"YOU ATE MY TRIX," I shouted.

"What? Are you going to let it ruin your whole day?"

Oh this was not the response I wanted to hear. I was *mad*. Mad that he ate my TRIX and even more mad that he did not seem to understand the magnitude of his criminal behavior. I immediately felt my face turn red and the vein in my forehead begin to throb (a trait I inherited from my father). I decided my answer was, YES. Yes I *was* going to let it ruin my whole day. And while I was at it, I was going to do my best to ruin *his* day too.

I stomped around the condo for the rest of the morning and then stomped around the office, where we both worked, too. I 'tskd' and grumbled and rolled my eyes. I ranted to my fellow employees about how awful the day was and I spent a good portion of the afternoon fuming. I asked Michael to do impossible tasks, knocked on his office door incessantly, bothering him with meaningless questions and nagging him to complete irrelevant tasks. Operation Ruined Day was actually progressing quite well until around 2 p.m., when I realized... I wasn't getting much done. And honestly, my bad mood was kind of starting to annoy me.

Wait.

Had I just surrendered *hours* of my life to an empty box of artificially sweetened children's cereal? Indeed I had. Even now, it sounds so ridiculous. Clearly I had lost all control of my mood, motivation and perspective. And while it would be easy to judge, I'm sure I'm not the first one who has lost a day to poor attitude management, and sadly, I'm sure I won't be the last.

• • • • •

Everyone has one: a day-ruining threshold. There are some who can be thrown off track by anything: oversleeping, crabby children, a negative email, and stolen cereal. Then there are others, a special few, the champions, who will be stopped by nothing. For those of us whose days can be ruined on a whim, we need to watch our (usually more successful) counterparts and learn from their attitude. And if that isn't good enough, I suggest enlisting a partner—a friend, a sister, a coach, a mentor (or in my case a fiancé)—*someone* who can stop us from losing precious time on insignificant issues. Someone whom we grant permission to say, "Really, are you going to let it ruin your whole day?" in the moments when we need the strength to snap out of it.

• • • • •

In the process of moving in with Michael, I lost many things. I lost most of my bathroom counter space, much of my closet space, all of my IKEA furniture and a little of my sanity. However, I gained something much more valuable than any of that: the security of knowing I would never ruin my own day.

That, and limited tooth decay ... because I haven't bought a box of TRIX since.

LOVE & LIQUID PINK CHALK

When I was little and was sick, my mom made me
buttered toast cut in four pieces. It was her secret cure.
It was as if she took a regular old piece of toast and
by cutting it in four, it took on special healing powers.
Toast-cut-in-four made being sick bearable.

Sadly, sometimes buttered toast just wasn't enough.
Sometimes the illness called for something more. I still
remember the slightly sympathetic face my mother wore
on these occasions when she had to ask me:

"Do you want some Pepto-Bismol?"

Ew. Gross.

I *hated* that stuff.

I knew I was seriously ill anytime she asked that question. I *had* to be. Seriously ill and slightly delirious, since there was nothing worse than drinking a tablespoon full of liquid pink chalk. Every time she mentioned it I would ask:

"Will it make me throw up?" Every little girl's worst nightmare.

"Well, if you don't *need* to throw up, it will just make you feel better. If you *do* need to throw up, it'll make you throw up. And *then* you'll feel better."

Sometimes I still hesitated. I tried holding out, waiting for the toast-cut-in-four to make the sickness go away. But alas, even as a little girl I knew that buttered toast was a fantasy solution. I knew that sometimes you had to endure pink chalk to get to the other side.

A couple times I felt better right away. A couple times, I threw up... but felt better shortly after.

It's a motto I've lived by ever since.

• • • • •

It was a pleasant Saturday morning and I was on a walk with a girlfriend; Starbucks in hand. We wore running shoes with no intention of running and sweat-wicking clothing with no intention of sweating. Instead, we caught up. We caught up on friends. We caught up on family. We caught up on married life (for me). We caught up on dating life (for her). We talked of world affairs, the global economy, the environment, and eventually back to her dating life.

After all. It was the most interesting of our topics.

My friend, a busy woman with no time for nonsense, had moved her search for an acceptable man off of the streets and local bars of her bustling city to an even *more* happening venue—online. Online dating.

I have to admit, I was a little jealous. I was just about to start dating online when I had met Michael. (I had also filled out my application for the show The Bachelor and just hadn't sent it in yet. I had every intention of being the girl who got along with all the ladies and didn't kiss the Bachelor until he asked me to marry him in the last episode. That, or, to be the one everyone hated. I could do that too).

My friend had been on several dates with different people who were supposedly "a match." Some were fine, one was awful, and one qualified as being better than she expected but not everything she dreamed. That particular guy was tall, kind of goofy, and Swedish.

I named him Sven.

After their initial online conversation, they got together once every two weeks or so for dinner. The conversation was OK but not overly stimulating. She found him interesting but not enthralling, good-looking but not entirely attractive, smart but kind of annoying. On the third date (six weeks into the "relationship") there was a kiss. Not an impressive kiss (he had skinny lips—perhaps it was a Swedish thing), but then again, a kiss isn't everything. And while she wasn't *overly* into it, she *could* be... if *he* was.

I was just about to do my Swedish chef impression to lighten the mood when....

At the exact moment I was throwing my first imaginary fish into the air....

My friend's face turned pale as she lifted her arm and

pointed.

And there, right on cue, was Sven. Tall, lanky, skinny-lipped Sven. Running right toward us.

It took a moment for them to *really* recognize each other, since it had been the standard two weeks since their last dinner. A mixture of shock, "What timing," and plain old "Do I know you?" crossed their faces and hung heavy on their words as they greeted each other. He was kind enough to slow down and I was wise enough to save my Swedish chef impression until later.

The three of us walked together for a bit. We talked of world affairs, the global economy, the environment. I tried to be funny so he would think, "Wow, this girl has funny friends." She tried to be cool so he would think, "Wow, this girl is cool." After about fifteen minutes we had run out of awkward things to say and he started running again. We continued walking with a more focused conversation on her dating life.

She went back and forth: Did he like her? Did she like him? Did that conversation go well? Would they be compatible? Should she call?Text?Email?Instant Message?Facebook?Tweet? No. No, no, no. It was his turn. She was pretty sure. Besides, he was the one with the skinny lips. She was the one who wasn't impressed. Right? Or was it him?

As we walked I could tell that this mystery was causing a growing feeling of angst for my dear, successful, grown woman friend. I wanted nothing more than to help her, but the only thing I could think of was:

If you want to know if he's interested, why don't you just *ask* him.

But I got the distinct feeling that was not the right thing to say; that it was something only a *married* friend would say. I was hoping I could get off the hook without having to say anything at all, but while the conversational pause lingered in the air, I knew I had to come up with something.

"Well, I think your only option is to drink the Pepto."

She stopped. She waited. She knew me well enough. She knew I was going somewhere with this. At least, she hoped.

"Here's the thing..." I started.

Too often we fool ourselves into believing that buttered toast-cut-in-four is going to get the job done when it comes to relationships. We make up excuses, we tell ourselves stories; we feed ourselves lies that are high in cholesterol and carbohydrates with very little nutritional value. We don't want to ask the questions and face the realities because we're afraid of the un-pleasantries. We want to avoid the vomit. But the truth of the matter is, by facing the issue head-on only one of two things can happen: 1) It goes well and you feel better, or 2) It goes poorly, you get sick, and you feel better. Take the Pepto. Ask the question you've been afraid to ask, make the move you've been afraid to make. Sure, you might have to endure some un-pleasantries, but in the end the fastest way to feeling better isn't in the comfort of bread and butter. It's in the Pepto.

Later that evening I got a text from my friend that read:

"Vomit."

It took me a minute, but I soon figured out exactly what she meant. She got up the courage, went the Pepto route, and asked Sven if he was really interested in see-ing her again to which he more or less replied....

No.

Unpleasant.

However, she was happy to report in subsequent texts that she already felt better now that she *knew* instead of just *wondering.*

Trust me when I say this; I have always been a buttered toast-cut-in-four kind of girl; but as I become more of the woman I want to be, I am more inclined to reach for the Pepto. And with my new adult perspective, liquid pink chalk has never tasted so good.

THE
SPONGE

We were having a domestic incident.

Michael was chasing me and I was screaming. It was
a blood-curdling, deep from the gut, heavy on the
shrill scream. Straight from the horror movies—fitting
because I was truly horrified. I raced into our bedroom
and was about to jump under the bed when Michael
came around the corner, weapon in hand. "No. Please,
I beg you. Don't. No. Please." I cried. I knew it would be
the end of me.

He let out an evil laugh, turned and walked back into
the kitchen. There, he went to work using the weapon to
clean the dishes.

I knew it would be the end of me.

He gave one last evil laugh, turned and walked back into the kitchen. There, he went to work using the weapon to clean the dishes.

A sponge.

A damp, dirty, smelly sponge.

I hate them. I won't use them. I won't touch them. I won't go near them. I. Hate. Sponges.
Foul Sponge Smell is my greatest weakness.
Yet strangely, weaknesses can sometimes be the best thing for you.

• • • • •

Every morning for about three years I took the same route to work. On that drive I passed a mountain and a zoo. I drove past desert botanical gardens and the stadium where the Oakland A's play during spring training. And while these were all very exciting, there was one other landmark on my drive to work that caught my attention every time I passed it.

The regional headquarters for the National Speakers

Association. NSA.

Every morning I saw the sign with their logo: The letters NSA and a microphone curling between them. It called to me, it taunted me. Every time I drove by it beckoned: "Kindra. I'm right here. I'm waiting." For three years I turned my head and kept driving.

What would I say to them? I asked myself. What would I say when I walked in the door? Hi. I'm Kindra.

(Actually, when I put it like that, it didn't sound *too* unreasonable.)

The ritual continued like this: Once I drove past NSA headquarters, I would spend the rest of my drive to work rehearsing what I might say should I decide to actually enter the building. I memorized my speaking résumé. I thought about my unique role in the speaker-scape and the diversity I could tell them I offer. I considered bringing a DVD of my previous work. I thought of witty yet intelligent things I could share with them so they would *know* they had a true gem on their hands. Perhaps they would even ask themselves "Where has she been for the past three years?!" I thought about what I might wear and how I would shake their hands as I walked in the door.

However, all of this mental rehearsing got me nowhere. After three years I always had a reason not to go in: my nails were chipped, my outfit didn't scream "speaker" that day, I was too busy, I was *way* too busy, I think they're closed today, I *had* to get to the office to check my email (that I just checked on my phone at the last red light). After three years never once did I flip on my blinker and take the quick right into the NSA parking lot because the *real* reason was: I was scared.

What if, after I showed them all I had to offer, it wasn't enough?

What then?

One afternoon in January, I met my friend Melissa for lunch. My fearless friend. When it came to business and putting yourself out there, the girl was wonder woman. I usually left lunch with Melissa feeling inspired and that afternoon was no different. I was driving back to the office with the on-top-of-the-world feeling that makes you forget to turn the radio on, when I saw it.

The NSA (curling microphone) sign.

"Today is the day," I thought to myself. Heck, I probably said it out loud. "I'm going in."

My nails were chipped. My hair was a little wind-blown because the convertible top was down (it was a warm January day). I was wearing a winter coat (because it was January, after all) that was making me a little sweaty (because it was Phoenix). I was nervous I still had a little lunch stuck in my teeth, but today was the day. I was determined. I flipped on my blinker, took the quick right, and pulled into the parking lot.

I stepped out of the car, walked to the front door and opened it. Only *then* did I realize I hadn't fully prepared my speech.

Crap. How was I going to impress them? What details should I include? I didn't have time think, before the girl behind the reception desk said hello. Despite the desire to run, I took a deep breath and gave the girl behind the desk my best handshake. She told me she was a temp and to wait while she found someone who could help me.

Shoot. I had just wasted my best handshake.

I sat in the lobby trying to look cool despite my nerves and the heat of my winter coat on a seventy-degree day, until a woman named Genevieve came out to greet me. I had never met a Genevieve before. I shook her hand.

It was an awkward shake. *Stupid temp stole my best handshake.* Nevertheless, she showed me to her office. I decided my strategy would be to *look* like I was listening as she told me about NSA, but all the while be rehearsing my résumé, my diverse role in the world of speakers, my witty and intelligent comments.

But as Genevieve spoke, I felt something in me relax, or sort itself out. Slowly I realized the real reason I had pulled into the lot instead of driving by the sign. Fortunately, at that moment Genevieve asked to know why I stopped in.

I knew *this* was my opportunity to impress her. To say something brilliant. And out of my mouth came this: "I want to be a sponge."

She was silent.

It wasn't my original plan, but I went with it. I explained that, while I know I have talent and while I know I have skill, I have a lot to learn about what it takes to be a professional speaker. The National Speakers Association would give me access to people who have the knowledge and experience I don't. "I simply want to sit, listen, learn, take notes, ask questions, and soak up as much

OTHERWISE UNTOLD { *A Collection of Stories Most People Would Keep to Themselves* }

as I can—as much as they are willing to offer. To be a
sponge."

I looked at Genevieve who smiled. She then offered a
statement that made the whole trip worthwhile.

"So many people come into an organization like this
with a goal to impress. They memorize their résumé and
talk about why they are unlike anything anyone has
seen. Honestly, those folks never make it very far. While
it is good to be confident, the true measure of this experience is not how impressive you are coming in—it's how
much you can learn while you are here; how impressive
you are when you walk *out*. And the members of this
association will help in whatever way they can to make
sure you get the information you seek."

At the end of our conversation, I shook Genevieve's hand
again—a good, natural, unrehearsed shake. I walked
out of the NSA office with a stack of information and
had to laugh a little. All that time I had been concerned
about how best to impress them with my *strength* when
what I really needed was my greatest weakness: a
sponge.

THE NEIGHBORHOOD DIRT

I never had neighbors growing up.

Sure, there were people who lived around us, and sometimes we called them neighbors, but we couldn't see them or hear them or smell them and they never gave us any trouble. The closest thing to trouble in our "neighborhood" was oversized goose droppings and gophers eating my mother's marigolds.

So when Michael and I moved out of our condo and into a little home in a sweet Phoenix neighborhood—a home with neighbors on all sides—I had some adjusting to do. I could see the cigarette smoke coming from the neighbors immediately to the north, hear the dogs barking from the neighbors immediately to the south, and smell the chickens (yes, *chickens*) from the neighbors immediately to the east—the neighbors across the alley.

The *crazy* neighbors.

• • • • •

One fall weekend, after an HGTV marathon, Michael and I decided to do some fence work to "create our unique outdoor sanctuary space." We painted our block fence to the south a bold purple and stained both sides of the wooden fence lining the alley "Natural Cedar," (natural cedar that comes in a can is the most natural of all the cedars). It was a tedious job (for Michael) and when it was finally complete, we both stood back and gazed upon our creation with pride. It was, hands down, the best-looking fence in the neighborhood.

Until....

Our back-alley neighbor, the one with the chickens, decided to do some HGTVing of his own. His particular project was, one could only assume, a Hole to China. Though I had missed that particular episode, he appeared to be fully inspired, removing a substantial amount of dirt from his yard. Dirt that had to go somewhere. Dirt that our back-alley neighbor decided to pile right up against our freshly painted masterpiece of a fence.

Not ideal.

Clearly, we were displeased. Aesthetically and environmentally displeased. The dirt was damaging our wood, making our fancy fence look sloppy, and the problem only got worse. Over the course of the weekend the dirt piled so high that one could walk along on top of it and peer effortlessly into our backyard, rendering our fence completely useless.

When Michael kindly brought this to the attention of the neighbor across the alley, the neighbor responded with several more wheelbarrows full of dirt up against our fence.

Michael, who rarely gets angry (even when, hypothetically, an individual tries to pick fights with him when in the mood for some drama), was not so kind the next time he saw the crazy back-alley neighbor. He made it clear that if the dirt dumping continued, he would have no choice but to call the authorities. Which authorities, he wasn't sure. But the authorities who were responsible for monitoring the neighborhood dirt would be notified.

With that, the illegal dumping ceased.

Until....

One afternoon we noticed, in our yard, about two feet from the fence, a small pile of dirt.
A perfect little pile deposited directly over the top of our artificial natural cedar fence.
Dirt that looked *just like* the dirt from our neighbor's yard.
But it couldn't be.... That was too absurd.

It had to have been left behind by the recent rain. Or from when Michael watered the palm trees we planted. Or maybe the garbage truck that drove up and down our back alley accidentally dumped a perfect little pile of dirt in our yard. We just couldn't imagine that someone would be *that* upset about a simple "please don't throw your dirt on our awesome fence" request.

And then it happened again.
It was a statement.
And again.
A threat.

And again.

We were being punished.

At least twice a week, it was there; a small shovel-sized pile of dirt resting squarely on our lawn, next to the landscape rock, two feet from the HGTVed fence. And it was clearly our back-alley neighbors; those chicken-loving jerks. Either the man with his bruised ego, the wife protecting her husband's honor, or the live-in grandma (old-lady grudges die hard).

Weeks worth of dirt passed. What started as an annoyance grew into a sense of unease, then fear, then fury. Who did they think they were terrorizing us like that? We simply wanted a clean fence. Was that too much to ask? I was ready to retaliate.

I wanted to throw the dirt back over their fence. Or put a pile of it in front of their gate—a "we know it's you" pile. I considered throwing a chicken breast over the wall after our research revealed that keeping chickens is illegal without written consent from all neighbors within 80 feet (and heck if we were gonna let the dirt slingers keep their pets). I even thought of knocking on their front door, acting all innocent, with a printed sign of one of the dirt piles and the words "Warning: Dirt Bandit on the Loose. Call 911 if Spotted" and then in smaller print, "let's send the monster to jail for life" just so they knew we were serious.

Michael said no to all of these ideas.

So I busied myself with other, more anonymous, activities.

I patrolled the backyard. Every half hour I made a note on a piece of paper: Dirt. No Dirt. Tracking the pattern of our attacker. I patrolled the alley. Looking for clues. Faking loud phone conversations that the crazy neighbors could most certainly hear, "Oh yeah, we've got all the evidence we need." I patrolled the block. I walked around to see whose car was in the drive when the dirt appeared. I patrolled from inside our home. I rearranged my desk so it looked out the back door and set up my Flip Cam and iPad in our back windows to record their every move as long as my batteries lasted.

I waited. For days, I waited. And though piles of dirt would appear, now with more frequency, I could never seem to catch them in the act. And then one morning, it happened.

At 10:43 A.M., 13 minutes *after* I had written "No Dirt" on my Dirt Tracker, and 10 minutes *before* I was going to change the battery on my dead Flip Cam, I was in the bedroom when I heard the irrefutable sound of a gate, slamming shut, in the alley.

I knew this was it. My time had come.

I bolted from the room to the back window and sure enough: DIRT! I let out a mighty roar, tore open our back door and raced, in my bra and panties (yes, we don't get dressed until after 11 A.M. in the Hall home) to the natural cedar fence. I jumped up onto the cheap wood panels and clung there like a cat on a curtain. I tried to catch a glimpse of the neighbor (the man, the woman, the grandma, whoever) walking back into the house but I was too late. There was no one there.

I cried out—a dramatic cry. Foiled again. I had missed my chance to spare my family more pain and now we were forced to live in fear for... heaven only knew how long. For a moment, I longed to be a child back in rural Minnesota; I longed for the days of no crazy neighbors, of the simpler problems like goose poop and marigold-eating gophers...

Wait.

I had a sudden flashback to my childhood and to the piles of dirt the gophers left behind as they dug their escape routes away from my mother's garden.

No.

It couldn't be. It *had* to be the crazy neighbors. They had a motive. The piles were shovel-sized. I had heard the gate slam just moments after the pile appeared. And we would have *seen* the *holes...* I mean, we *had* looked for *holes.... Hadn't* we? I slowly walked over to the pile of dirt, cautiously lowered my head to get a better angle, and sure enough found myself staring down a dark, gopher-sized tunnel.

Well what do you know.
Gophers.

• • • • •

Even though the threat was never *real*, standing there on our beautiful lawn surrounded by our pristine fences in my unmentionables, I felt relief wash over me. Though the gopher killed two of our palm tress, one of our sprinklers, and caused months of slight, nagging fear, I was relieved to know we were safe. And relieved, I suppose, that if crazy neighbors were inevitable, at least *we* were the craziest of them all.

Suddenly aware that my perfectly sane neighbors may start talking if I didn't put some clothes on, I walked back into the house and called Michael. He didn't answer. So I left him a message: I had solved the Dirt Mystery.

Those crazy neighbors were throwing gophers over our fence.

PARADISE FOUND

I love birthdays. Especially mine. After waiting an entire year, my birthday was finally back and I decided to celebrate all week. I used the phrase "It's my birthday!" liberally, shouting it out in the grocery store, in restaurants, and as a way to greet people on the phone when they called me. I enjoyed a multitude of "birthday" dinners and used the "but it's my birthday" excuse to get out of a number of household chores. I did such a good job extending the celebration of my birthday it could very well have been the best birthday *ever* except for one, small detail.

Twenty-nine. I was turning twenty-nine.

In a phone conversation, my mother asked me how I felt about the fact that I was turning twenty-nine. My answer was simple.

Yuk.

"Let me be clear," I explained. "I have no problem with getting older. In fact, the problem is I would rather be turning *thirty*." I paused. My mother didn't respond so I continued. "I feel like I've been here a long time. I feel like I have the wisdom, the maturity, the spirit of someone who is turning thirty. I'm ready to move into the next decade of ages. I'm ready for the big celebration that comes when you leave a decade behind. I'm ready to exit my twenties. Therefore, twenty-nine," I explained, "is kind of anticlimactic."

There was silence on the other line. I prepared myself for the typical "Youth is wasted on the young," or "Enjoy your twenties while you still have them" responses. But those words never came. Instead, my mother said in her contemplative voice (that I hope to one day master but I'm pretty sure I'll have to be much farther along than thirty):

"Twenty-nine was my most difficult birthday, too. But for

very different reasons."

Here were the reasons she gave me.

My mother and father got married when she was 22. At age 26 she had a (very, very, very beautiful) daughter— me. At age 28 she had a son. Therefore, the birthdays leading up to twenty-nine looked something like this: Twenty-two. World at her feet. Marrying the man of her dreams. Whole life ahead of her; a life of adventure and romance. Twenty-six. The wonder, the magic of a first pregnancy. The belly, the baby talk, there could be nothing better. Twenty-eight. Second pregnancy. The joy of a growing family. The excitement of a son, of a full home. Then she turned 29. And that was that.

While she loved her husband and adored her children, she couldn't escape the feeling that something wasn't right. That something was *missing*. Where was the adventure? Where was the romance, now that the excitement of the changes in her life had settled?

Was this it?

Twenty-nine. Work. Wife. Mom. Work. Wife. Mom. She didn't remember signing up for this. This wasn't the

Paradise she had planned. She felt lost—like the thing
that was missing was *her*.

A day that should have been a celebration of her life,
and instead she felt like she had none. Twenty-nine, she
explained, was anticlimactic... at best.

I had never known this story of my mother. And hearing it
reminded me of a different story. A story I first heard on a
recording by storyteller Steve Sanfield; a story retold here
as I remember it, with his blessing. A story called *Could
This Be Paradise?*

• • • • •

There once was a man who was displeased with his life.
Every morning at the kitchen table, over a lukewarm
breakfast, he would scorn his life that had fallen short
of his expectations. He didn't like his work, his wife was
a nag, and his children could never be satisfied. Since
it didn't appear that his lot would be changing anytime
soon, he spent most of his time dreaming of Paradise.
"Someday, someday I will journey to Paradise."

Then, one day, not much different than any other day he
decided *this* would be the day he traveled to Paradise.
Without a word to his wife, without a hug to his children,

he pushed open the heavy front door, walked through the front gate with a broken latch and down the street to the village he had called home.

He passed the people who knew him by name, little did they know this would be the last time they saw him. He walked by the general store, the town hall, and the church. The buildings were old and tattered. He was happy to be trading them in for the beautiful buildings of Paradise. It didn't take long until he was at the bottom of the hill that marked the edge of his village. He took one last, lingering look—for this was certainly the last time his eyes would ever see this town. He was a man bound for Paradise.

The man climbed the hill and began his journey. He crossed the countryside, traveled in the direction of the sun, certain it would bring him to Paradise. However, Paradise was not a mere day's travel. Eventually the sun slipped beneath the horizon, the sky deepened and the chill of night fell. The man decided to stop for the evening. He found a tree that would provide sufficient shelter, and before lying down, removed his shoes. The man carefully placed his shoes beside the tree, pointed in the direction he had been traveling, pointed them toward Paradise. With that, he for the night and began dreaming of the Paradise that awaited him.

• • • • •

Whether as a joke, a prank, or to teach the man a lesson
it is not clear. What *is* clear is that night while the
traveler slept a troll came along and, without a sound,
took the man's shoes and turned them around. The
shoes now pointed back in the direction from which the
Paradise-seeker had come. With that, the troll vanished.

• • • • •

As the first rays of the morning fell, the man awoke.
"Today is the day I find Paradise!" He leapt to his feet,
put on his shoes, and began traveling in the direction
they told him to go—traveling toward Paradise.

After nearly an entire day of walking, he arrived. "Paradise!" he shouted from a top the hill that marked the
edge of Paradise. As he stared at the village below, he
thought it looked vaguely familiar. "Strange," he said.
"It looks similar to my old village." The man didn't think
much of it; he was too excited to have finally found
Paradise. He descended the hill.

As he walked, he passed a church, a town hall, and a
general store. "Strange," he thought, "these buildings

look as tattered as the buildings in my old village." Writing it off as a coincidence, he kept on walking, thrilled to be in Paradise. As he walked, he met the people of Paradise. Strangely, they knew him by name.

The man continued until he came to the end of the road where there was a gate with a broken latch. He walked through, and as he did, he heard a voice calling him in for dinner. "Strange, she sounds just like my old wife." But never having turned down dinner before, he entered the home. As he opened the heavy front door, he was greeted by two children who wrapped themselves around him, happy to have their loved one home.

For every morning after, the man sat at that kitchen table over a lukewarm breakfast, content with his life in Paradise. Or at least, he was pretty sure it was Paradise. If not, it was close enough.

• • • • •

I don't personally remember much about my mother's twenty-ninth birthday—I was just shy of three years old after all.

I *do* know she never left our home or our village. She probably opened gifts that she bought for herself and gave to my well-meaning father to wrap and give back to her. She probably cleaned the kitchen-turned-battlefield after her two children "baked her a cake." She probably spent most of the day in the role of "mother" and "wife" and not much time as "the birthday girl." She probably called her mom and told her that her twenty-ninth birthday was... anticlimactic.

As the day came to a close, she probably tucked the kids in, kissed her sleeping husband good night, removed her shoes, and crawled into bed. And in those last moments before sleep took her away for the night, perhaps she dreamed of Paradise....

• • • • •

If I've learned anything in my twenty-nine-plus years, it is that the desire for Paradise is not itself a crime. Everyone desires Paradise. The confusion of where to *find* Paradise is where the problem lies. Paradise is a choice. It is a state of mind. Paradise doesn't exist unless you create it, unless you *choose* it. The next time you seek Paradise, long for it, fear you may never find it, turn your shoes around and walk back to where it all starts. With you.

My mother awoke on her second day of being twenty-nine to two children wrapped around her, a husband who adored her, and a renewed perspective. In the night, someone had come and turned her shoes around. It wasn't a troll, it was *her.* She chose to see the Paradise around her.

After my conversation with my mother, I decided to approach my twenty-ninth year differently. I decided to celebrate, not scorn, the fact that that I had exactly that many years under my belt: no more, no less. Thrilled to have exactly what I had, and thrilled to be exactly where I was. Paradise.

SAND

There are many things to love about Coronado, California.

There is the bridge. There is the Del. There is Danny's Burgers. There is the little yellow house by Star Park where *The Wizard of Oz* books were written. There is the view of San Diego. And of course, there is the beach.

But of all these things to love about the island, my *favorite* thing is the morning.

Michael and I often head back to the island to stay with his parents and escape the everyday responsibilities that lurk around every corner of our home. Each morning I wake up in Coronado, Michael rolls over and says, "Let's go get coffee." We put on various layers of clothes, our tennis shoes, walk downstairs, out the door, and begin the twelve-block walk to Starbucks. Every morning

Michael waits in line for his coffee and I walk next door
to the bakery where I get a crispy-flaky-sugar-coated
pastry disk. Then, with our goodies in hand, we take the
"long way home."

The long way home involves walking down Orange Avenue, through the Hotel Del, and then along the beach.
Some days we walk in the sand and others we take the
sidewalk. When we run out of shoreline, we wander our
way back home taking different routes to admire the
many houses that give the island its charm.

Three hours later, our walk-to-get-coffee is complete.

Holidays are no different.

It was the day after Christmas and we were in the
middle of our Coronado morning routine. Michael
had his coffee, I had already finished my crispy disk,
we were finished at the Del, and we were walking the
sidewalk that framed the famous beach. Despite a chill
in the air, the sun was out and people from all over the
world were *also* out on the sidewalk that framed the
famous beach—young couples, old couples, couples with
children, joggers, walkers, dog people. It was a little
crowded, but festive and cheerful.

As we maneuvered our way down the sidewalk, two children stood out. They were a young sister and brother who had obviously been told to wait by the lamppost while their parents rummaged around in the minivan parked next to them. To entertain themselves the children were playing a game they had just created, a game I assumed was called, "This is My Pile of Sand." They took turns standing on the tiny piles of sand that had accumulated on either side of the lamppost. The sister would yell, "This is MY pile of sand," and the brother would run to her side, stick his foot in the pile and yell, "No! This is MY pile of sand!" The sister would then run to the other side of the lamppost, stand in the tiny pile on that side and yell, "This is MY pile of sand."

I watched these barefooted children battle each other as we walked. It was all out war. They fought hard and loudly just to wiggle their tiny toes in "piles of sand" not much bigger than ant hills. Nothing could break their focus, not even their mother yelling to play nicely.

As we passed the children, I couldn't help but look to my left....

There, filling the two hundred yards between the sidewalk and the sea, sprawling miles down the waterscape in sheets of winter cold-glistening white, were limitless *tons* of classic California *sand*.

Some was spotted with footprints from tourists, some lay smooth, and still more lay in waves—textured by the wind. Finally, immediately in front of where the children were playing "This is My Pile of Sand," towered the Coronado Dunes; dunes that were big enough to exhaust a high school water polo team forced to run them during early morning practice. Dunes that would sort the men from the boys during Navy SEAL training. Dunes that, from the sky, clearly spell the word C-O-R-O-N-A-D-O.

Enormous piles of sand. Just a few feet from where the children played. *Soaring* piles of sand to satisfy their every sand-filled dream. Piles the children never even *noticed* because they were too busy fighting over the tiny accumulations around the base of the lamppost where they stood.

They never even looked up. The thought never even *occurred* to them that more sand could be waiting just *moments* away on the other side of the concrete path.

Now, to their credit, they were children—children who were no doubt told by their parents not to so much as *look* in the direction of the beach. They were children who had no choice but to keep themselves busy while waiting for their parents to take them by the hand and lead them to their next adventure. They did the best they could with what they had without being tempted by what was around them.

They were children.
But what is *my* excuse?

On more than one occasion I have found myself entirely wrapped up, fighting and frustrated, stomping around barefoot trying to stake my claim on a tiny, insignificant pile of sand—the sand of relationships, the sand of social status or money, the sand of a career... whatever. I have been deeply consumed in games of King of the Mini Mound that leave me oblivious to the beautiful beaches around me. Beaches with unlimited sand, possibility, and happiness. We've all been there. Investing our energy in small things while the big ones lay untouched on the other side of the sidewalk.

As Michael and I walked past the children, I lost myself in these thoughts. Startled by my silence (an unusual occurrence), he asked what was on my mind and I told him about the dueling brother and sister and their tiny piles of sand and about how ashamed I was that I am sometimes one of them. He nodded. He was too.

Shortly after passing the children, the sidewalk became a little too crowded for us "natives" (I figure when you marry a native you *become* one) and we strayed from the shoreline. We began weaving our way back through the Coronado grid—streets of letter and number. As we wandered, passing block after block of gorgeous houses built by dreams realized, we talked about the beaches of sand waiting for *us,* beaches we might not have noticed, beaches it was time to explore.

And we talked about the tiny piles of lamppost sand it was time to leave behind.

By the time we turned the corner onto the block we called home for the weekend, the sun was high and the day was warming up. Afternoon was approaching. It was time to say goodbye to another morning—my favorite thing about Coronado—and to look forward to the many mornings, spent on vast beaches, ahead.

DOROTHY & A HEAP OF YELLOW BRICKS

I spent much of my childhood as Dorothy.

I had the light-blue checkered dress. I had a small, brown stuffed dog who I called Toto (I actually *still* have the small, brown stuffed dog, and she *still* sleeps in my bed). I had a basket for Toto that was supposed to be for the toilet paper in the bathroom. I had some black patent shoes that my mother and I soaked in glue and covered in red glitter. I had the Rainbow song down. I had the yellow-brick-road skip perfected. And I nailed the instrumental "ree-ii-deet-dee-dee-dee-dee-dee" portion of the *Off to See the Wizard* number every time.

For four consecutive Halloweens, I was Dorothy and one

year I made my family join in; Dad was the Tin Man, Mom was the Scarecrow, little brother was the Lion, and my sister was a Carebear (we ran out of Oz costumes). Every year I wore the same Dorothy dress. Every year my Dorothy got a little more inappropriate as I grew and the dress didn't.

Every year for Christmas we made ornaments. My brother made Christmas trees, my sister made candy canes. I made Dorothys.

The neighbor's garden was my poppy field. And everywhere I went, I searched for the yellow brick road. I spent many late afternoons standing at the top of the hill overlooking our swooping, rural, Minnesota back yard, alone. Searching. And as the sun set, the grass, the trees, the sky, the lake, the *world* as I knew it turned a unique Midwest-gold color. I carefully scanned the scene for evidence of yellow bricks that could carry me to my destiny. I knew they were there, I just could never find them. Secretly I feared that made me a pretty miserable excuse for a Dorothy.

Then, on my fifth birthday, I received the *best* gift my Dorothy heart could ask for; two tickets to the local community theater production of *The Wizard of Oz*.

Whoa.

I wasn't even sure what a play *was*, but I knew it meant
I was going to *see* Dorothy. I was going to *see* Toto and
Glinda and the munchkins. I was *going to OZ*. And *I
trembled with excitement when I realized I was finally
going to see the yellow brick road.*

When the day of the play finally came, I Dorothy-
skipped around the house screaming "I'm off to see the
Wizard, the Wonderful Wizard of Oz because because
because because BECAAAAUUUSSE...." That night I
put on my too-short Dorothy dress, my black shoes that
left a trail of red glitter, grabbed Toto and tied a leash
around her neck, clicked my heels and I was ready.

I remember sitting in the theater before the show began.
It was packed with people and a growing murmur of
excitement—community theater at its finest. My mother
and I were on the aisle about twelve rows from the stage.
I was talking to her. Nonstop. Very loudly. I had many
questions. Will the tornado hurt us? What do flying
monkeys eat? Is that man in front of us with no hair a
munchkin? She answered all of them, she always did,
but in a hushed tone. Just as I was about to inquire
where I could get my own floating bubble, the room went

dark, the curtains opened, and the show began.

It was *magic*.

I saw Auntie Em and Uncle Henry. Mrs. Gulch rode
in on her bike (and almost right into a barn that was
plywood painted by high school kids, but Uncle Henry
grabbed her bike basket just in time). Toto was there
and only peed on the stage once. I cowered in my seat as
the tech crew banged on pieces of metal backstage and
the light crew flashed the lights a few times to simulate
a tornado. I adored the children dressed as munchkins
and the adults who squatted around trying to *look* like
munchkins. When Glinda arrived in her billowing pink
prom dress and crown (rolled out on a platform with
wheels by the stage crew dressed in all black and blow-
ing bubbles), I thought I had died and gone to five-year-
old girl heaven. And when the green woman in a witch
hat with an evil cackle took the stage in a sad little puff
of paprika, I hid my eyes behind my stuffed Toto until
she was gone.

And then there was Dorothy.

Oh Dorothy. She was as beautiful as I had remembered
in her blue-checkered dress. I sang along to every

word as she stood by the wagon with hay and sang *Somewhere Over the Rainbow* (except for the weird lyrics at the beginning of the song that were cut out of the movie so no one knows, or cares, about them). I nodded in agreement as she noted she wasn't in Kansas and I gasped as she put the ruby slippers on her feet.

They were real rubies. It was *all* real.

I sat quietly in my seat, mesmerized.

That is.
Until.
Glinda pointed her wand to the floor of the stage and said in a voice as sweet as the curls in my pigtails,

"Follow the Yellow Brick Road."
The munchkins repeated the sentiment.
"Follow the Yellow Brick Road."
Everyone on the stage was pointing to the floor....
"Follow the Yellow Brick Road."

And there was *nothing* there.

No bricks. No stones. No paint. No brick-shaped-stickers. Not even a few pieces of yellow and orange construc-

tion paper. Nothing that even *resembled* a Yellow Brick
Road.

I frantically looked around the theater—to the people
sitting around me, to the munchkin-man sitting in front
of me, to my mother who brought me there in the first
place. Was no one going to say anything? Did no one
else see something very, *very* wrong with this picture? I
knew I had to do something.

I stood up in my chair and shouted in my loudest outside voice:

"THERE IS NO YELLOW BRICK ROAD!"

Everything stopped. The actors fell silent. Everyone
turned. Everyone stared at the three-foot-tall Dorothy in
a miniskirt holding a stuffed dog on a rope in one hand
and an angry finger pointed to the stage with the other.

Yeah. I blew that wide open.

• • • • •

More than once I have felt this way—like there's *supposed* to be a yellow brick road, and like other people
are following it, and like I'm the only one who is staring

at an empty stage with a bunch of people in costume pointing at a phantom path. Part of the reason I loved being Dorothy was because it seemed so easy. I knew all I had to do was *find* the yellow brick road and then *follow* it to the Emerald City. Skip and dance and meet friends along the way, maybe get hit in the head with an apple or two, get a makeover and I'd be there. My destiny.

How was I supposed to get where I was going in life if there was no yellow brick road?

· · · · ·

After the outburst, my mother placed a graceful hand on my shoulder and helped me back into my seat. She leaned over to whisper that it was OK, it would be OK. I whispered back (with five-year-old-whisper volume) with genuine concern, If there was no yellow brick road how do Dorothys ever meet the wizard? There, in a dark theater, while mediocre actors made their way down a nonexistent road, my mother leaned over and spoke in a way that only mothers can.

"Sweet Kindra. Most Dorothys have to find their *own* way to the Emerald City. Real life Dorothys *create* the yellow brick road with their imaginations."

303

I sat back in my seat, trying to take it all in. For the rest of Act 1 and all of Act 2, though I had waited a lifetime to see that glowing golden road, I had no choice but to use my imagination to make the Land of Oz the place I knew it to be.

When the show was over we walked into the post-show chaos in the lobby where, as if he had been waiting for her, the Scarecrow jumped out and hugged my mom. She hugged him back, told him she loved the show, and then introduced me....

I couldn't speak. I stood there, my jaw on the ground, Toto dropping from my arm and hanging lifeless, inches off the floor, from her leash.

My mom never told me she was friends with *The Scarecrow*. (I think he was her chiropractor).

He took one look at the starstruck little Dorothy, swooped me up in his arms, and took off running, yelling back to my mom, "She needs to meet Dorothy!" His straw was scratchy on my legs as he raced down flights of stairs. My head was bouncing and glitter was flying off my shoes as we made our way to the dressing rooms. He pounded on the door yelling "Dorothy! Dorothy!"

just like Uncle Henry did during the tornado. The door opened and there. she. was. Illuminated by the glow of twelve light bulbs framing the mirror next to where she stood. Dorothy turned to look at me... and everything made sense.

She wasn't wearing her Dorothy dress, she was in jeans. Her ruby slippers had been replaced with tennis shoes and her curly locks had been pulled into a haphazard ponytail. She was nothing like I expected her to be. There was no magic, no sparkle, just a girl with pretty brown hair, a nice smile, and a kind voice.

I thought, "If *she* can make it to the Emerald City with no yellow brick road...."

We made some Dorothy-to-Dorothy small talk until The Scarecrow brought me back to my mom, I said goodbye to the Land of Oz, and we went home.

• • • • •

I am still Dorothy.
I am still journeying to the Emerald City, seeking my destiny. I have danced, skipped, sung songs, and traveled with an unlikely crew of characters who would do anything for my happiness. I have fought flying mon-

keys, been lost in the forest, had apples tossed at my
head, and fallen asleep when I should have been forging
onward. I have also come face to face with the Wicked
Witch, who tries to rob me of the future I desire. But for
me, and all real-life Dorothys who wear jeans, tennis
shoes, and haphazard ponytails, the greatest obstacle to
my happiness is not some woman in a pointed hat with
an unbecoming cackle.

The greatest obstacle... is *me*.

With every moment of self-doubt, every hour of procras-
tination, I watch my skin turn various shades of green.
I see the words painted across my sky and hear them
echo inside my head, "Surrender Dorothy," and though
I *wish* all it took was a bucket of water to make the
problem melt away, I don't live in the Land of Oz.

Where I live, there is no yellow brick road waiting to
be found and followed. And as a real-life Dorothy, I've
stopped searching for it. That is something silly little
girls do. Instead, I carry with me a heap of yellow bricks.
I create the golden road as I go.

Acknowledgements

A little coffee can go a long way.

It can eventually become a book.

For that, I must first and foremost thank Chrissy and Mark Donnelly. I'll never forget that very first morning at coffee, nervously pouring my heart out to you – telling you my stories, not sure what would come of it all. I will be forever grateful for your guidance, for your friendship, for your patience, but most of all, for your faith in me. I started this book because you believed I could – I finished it because I began to believe in myself. For much of that, I have you to thank.

I learned to tell stories as a child by listening to the best storyteller there is. Donald Davis, thank you for your teaching – face to face or from the stage, you are the reason I experience life the way I do – as a story waiting to be told.

I had the privilege of working with an incredible team. Thank you Peter Tepp for your editing and to Sarah Sandhaus of Electric Dreams Design for making this book beautiful. A big thank you to my team of early readers: Sarah Valentine, Denise Shorall, Ana Auther, Stephanie Sauerbry Louis, Samantha Dunn, David Wintersteen, Patrick McGrane, Daran Grimm, Karri Kelly, Millie Jackson, Maren Misner, Andrea Waltz, John Maus, Jim Sauerbry, Katie Owen, Melissa Jill Hester, Catherine Lanigan, and Darren Hardy. Your observations shaped this book. Without your thoughtful comments and dedicated reviews, this project would not be what it is today. Thank you for your honesty, your wisdom, and your excitement.

Thank you to storyteller Steve Sanfield for sharing your version of Could this be Paradise? in Jonesborough that I could hear it years later. And thank you for your permission to share my version of your version here.

Finally, thank you to my family and friends for letting me tell (my version of) these stories. Thank you Michael for your support and for being such a great literary character.

About the Author

Kindra Hall lives in Phoenix, Arizona where Thursday night is Date Night and Sunday morning she teaches spin class at Studio 360. She and Michael have a son and, if you're reading this after mid-September 2012, a daughter too.